Leading with Emotion

Reaching Balance in Educational Decision Making

James O. McDowelle
and
Kermit G. Buckner

A ScarecrowEducation Book

The Scarecrow Press, Inc.
Lanham, Maryland, and Oxford
2002

A SCARECROWEDUCATION BOOK

Published in the United States of America
by Scarecrow Press, Inc.
A Member of the Rowman & Littlefield Publishing Group
4720 Boston Way, Lanham, Maryland 20706
www.scarecroweducation.com

PO Box 317
Oxford
OX2 9RU, UK

British Library Cataloguing in Publication Information Available

Library of Congress Cataloging-in-Publication Data

Buckner, Kermit G.
Leading with emotion : reaching balance in educational decision making / Kermit Buckner, James O. McDowelle.
p. cm.
"A ScarecrowEducation book."
Includes bibliographical references.
ISBN 0-8108-4410-9 (alk. paper) — ISBN 0-8108-4411-7 (pbk. : alk. paper)
1. Educational leadership. 2. School management and organization. 3. Emotional intelligence. I. McDowelle, James O. II. Title.

LB2806 .B84 2002
371.2—dc21

2002070

∞™ The paper used in this publication meets the minimum requirements of American National Standard for Information Sciences—Permanence of Paper for Printed Library Materials, ANSI/NISO Z39.48-1992.
Manufactured in the United States of America.

Contents

Introduction

Both of the authors of this book have spent the better part of our professional lives either as school leaders or working with school leaders as advisors, teachers, or in some other capacity. During our careers, we have both come across excellent literature on school leadership and administration, but we harbored the suspicion that something was missing in all of that great literature. The writings on leadership in the schools certainly covered the rational, analytic, reflective aspects of the leader's life. But they didn't quite capture the emotional, sometimes irrational, and often even zany side of running schools and school systems. In short, the whole spectrum of behavior and emotions are encountered when working with people. We believe working with people to be the most important aspect of school leadership. We also believe the concept of emotional intelligence provides new insight about human behavior and thus becomes the missing ingredient in studying school leadership and determining who will succeed and who will fail while working with people.

This book is an attempt to incorporate the latest research on human behavior and the emotions, particularly research on emotional intelligence, with the latest research on school leadership. We have structured the book so we can view this research and leadership itself from three perspectives. First, the perspective of the leader; second, the perspective of constituents with whom the leader is working; and third, from the perspective of the specific situation with which the leader is confronted. Case studies, events taken from recent news accounts, and behavioral and neurological research are described to illustrate the importance of the emotions in leadership. We have frequently focused on situations that occur in school leadership that have a particular emotional potential, such as dealing with ethical and moral problems, working with issues of diversity, and leading during periods of change. We believe the ability to handle emotion-laden situations of this nature separates the successful leader from the unsuccessful leader.

At the end of each chapter, five fundamental facts cited within the chapter are provided to aid school leaders in integrating and applying the information. Explanations of the research and concepts are placed in the nitty-gritty environment in which school leadership occurs. The book uses real-world examples to demonstrate how emotional intelligence can be applied during periods of change and/or while acting as an instructional leader. This book is devoted to developing those intangible qualities that enable a leader to know and manage his emotional stability and engender emotional awareness and assurance in others.

The basic premise of the book is that leadership skills, such as communication, motivation, conflict resolution, team building, and persuasion are based in the emotions. Emotion plays a pivotal role in using these abilities. Therefore, we must understand the role of the emotions and the importance of emotional intelligence to effectively exercise these skills. New research on the role of the emotions in cognitive processing forces us to reassess our assumptions about human nature. This research asserts that emotions are a fundamental part of the cognitive process. In the past, emotion and reason were thought of as separate entities. This new research causes us to elevate the importance of the emotions in our behavior and decision making. We all agree that too much emotion can hinder decision making. It has now been found that the absence of emotion can also hamper the decision-making process. Consequently, emotional intelligence, the ability to process information about the emotions and use this information to manage your own emotions and the emotions of others, is rapidly coming to be viewed as an important concept in the leadership literature. We have tried to write a book that would have helped us when we began our careers as school leaders and would help reconceptualize the role of school leader if we were in that position now. We hope you will find the book helpful and occasionally enjoyable.

CHAPTER 1

What the Book Is All About: Defining Emotional Intelligence

This is a book about leadership in public and private schools. Although a number of books have been written on the subject, we believe this book is different. Many authors open the discussion of leadership by listing the varied opinions about the primary focus and function of school leadership. We do not agree with this technique. We believe there is one clear, primary focus for school leadership and one simple, overriding function. For us, the primary focus for school leadership is people and the overriding function of school leadership is working with and through people in a productive capacity.

RESEARCH ON HUMAN NATURE

If the fundamental heart and purpose of school leadership is people and productive interactions with them, it follows that possessing knowledge about the basic nature of men and women is essential to success as a school administrator. In the past decade, cognitive and neurological research have offered findings that can change how we perceive the fundamental nature of humankind. These findings are based on more than eighty years of work by neurologists, biologists, cognitive scientists, and others interested in how the mind works and on the role of the emotions in thinking and behavior. If we accept this research, we must also change how we think about working with people. The purpose of this book is to apply this research to school leadership. After reading this book, you will have an understanding of the skills and knowledge needed to apply the latest neurocognitive research to the interpersonal skills of school leadership. We contend that interpersonal skills are the most essential skills for the school leader.

Traditional and Emerging Views of Human Nature

Traditionally, humans were viewed as rational beings subject to irrational or emotional flights of fancy that were usually harmful or, at best, nonproductive. Recent research by neurologists, biologists, and cognitive scientists turned these notions of reason and emotion upside down (for a more complete description, see Further Readings on Neurocognitive Research at the end of this book).

Research on the brain indicates that the emotions are just as important as reason in the decision-making process. In fact, without the interaction of the emotions and reason, rational thought is greatly limited. New assertions about how the mind works are challenging old assumptions about how we think and act. Social scientists often cite the concept of *rational man* to support many economic, political, and leadership theories. The rational man concept is a theoretical model of how people behave in certain situations. The concept is based on the belief that people make logical, rational choices based on their own or somebody else's self-interest. The concept assumes a cold, objective approach to decision making and omits the role of the emotions and subjective perceptions.

We think this is a limited and ultimately distorted view of the way people act and work. The rational model of decision making is also contradicted by new research about how the brain functions. Although most of these findings have been published in the last decade, the approach to leadership suggested by this research is not totally new. Many experienced leaders know that they must consider the emotions of their constituents when exercising leadership. Good leaders know that when working with people toward change, no matter how incremental the change might be, they must first deal with the emotions of anxiety and fear before they can articulate the logical and rational components of the change. In attempting to resolve conflicts arising in any organizational setting, experienced leaders know they must first deal with the emotions underlying the conflict before dealing with the factual aspects of the dispute. If the emotional elements of the conflict are ignored, it is extremely difficult to focus the contending parties on the objective aspects of the disagreement.

The example below contrasts the traditional and emerging views of how the mind works and the role of the emotions in decision making.

Old Assumptions	New Assertions
Emotions are separate and lower neurological operations.	Emotion and reason work together in decision making with the emotions having the dominant role.
Reason controls the emotions.	Emotion directs reason to the problem to be solved.
Emotion impedes rational thought.	Uncontrolled emotions impede rational thought, but a lack of emotion/reason interaction also impedes rational thought.

Human Nature and School Leadership

A growing body of research pinpoints a lack of understanding of human nature as a major reason for failures in leadership in general and school leadership in particular. Limited understanding of human nature leads to an inability to exercise effective interpersonal skills in motivation, communication, persuasion, team building, and conflict resolution.

All of these skills require sensitivity or knowledge about the emotions. Superintendents fail not because they do not have the technical skills of budgeting or planning, but because they cannot work in productive ways with constituents, including teachers, parents, students, and board members. Principals fail not because they cannot understand school policy, but because they cannot understand and make reasonable predictions about human behavior (see Further Readings on Leadership Failure).

The following recent, real-life example supports the need for highly developed interpersonal skills.

THE DESCARTES MIRACLE

Tommy Glick hit the ground running as the new principal of Descartes Elementary. He quickly decided that in the era of high-stakes testing, when test scores were published twice a year for each individual school in local newspapers, raising test scores should become the main priority for his new school. The superintendent of schools, Dr. Spock, confirmed Glick's belief that test scores were the top priority. The superintendent felt that Descartes's demographic make-up indicated that the students could do much better on the state tests and that the previous principal had simply not been aggressive enough in establishing priorities for the school.

Encouraged, even emboldened, by his superintendent, Tommy convened a group of teachers to develop a plan to raise test scores. Unfortunately, as the team laid out the broad direction of the plan and moved to hash out the details, Tommy began to work on his own without consulting with the rest of the group. He had not meant to exclude the teachers from the development of the plan; it just seemed the writing of the plan went so much smoother and faster when he worked alone. In fact, Tommy was extremely knowledgeable about curriculum and instruction and the plan was very well thought out. Tommy Glick also created an effective PowerPoint presentation for his teachers, staff, and school community that described his plan to raise test scores. The presentation gave a detailed description of the current status of Descartes's test scores and delineated precisely how scores could be raised. Tommy's plan called for massive curriculum realignment, extensive drills in test-taking skills, and more time on task in each classroom. The presentation was articulate, logical, and coherent. Parents at each presentation were impressed. Teachers were likewise impressed by Tommy's knowledge of curriculum and instruction but a little concerned about their minimal role in developing the plan. Still, the teachers were swayed by Glick's enthusiasm and certainty.

At the end of the school year, test scores had not only been raised but were now the highest in the school system at the elementary level. The parents at Descartes were proud of their school and their children. The superintendent was happy. Tommy Glick was not only very, very happy but also proud. Tommy was so proud, in fact, that he began to conduct workshops about what he liked to call the *Descartes Miracle*. Tommy's workshops were a brilliant exposition of the principal's role in raising test scores. Tommy was so busy conducting his workshops and granting media interviews he did not notice that his teachers were not quite as pleased with the school's success as the rest of the Descartes's constituencies. In the teacher's lounge, they began to discuss the old (and better) days when the Descartes curriculum allowed them more time for divergent thinking skills such as creativity and literary synthesis. They began to reminisce about the times when they had more freedom to exercise their own teaching creativity.

Some of this talk spilled over into the parent network, particularly those parents who spent a lot of time in school—in other words, some of the most active parents in the school. Because most of the teachers at Descartes were competent professionals and meant the best for the children and the school, eventually a delegation of teachers went to see Tommy Glick to share their concerns. Unfortunately, Tommy had received little training in the most important aspect of communication: listening. Tommy did not hear the serious discontent masked by the teachers' observations. Tommy therefore responded to the teachers' concerns with selected extracts of his workshops about the *Descartes Miracle*. The teachers did not actually consider what had happened a miracle. They thought it was the result of focused effort and a lot of their hard work. A few parents also began to express concerns to Tommy about what they considered an overemphasis on testing. Soon, teachers and parents began to form small, but lethal, alliances of the discontented.

Meanwhile, Tommy, who was extremely busy, occasionally made an error in judgment while disciplining a child or reprimanding a teacher. He was vaguely aware of these minor mistakes but felt they did not matter in the overall scheme of things because he was the main reason for the *Descartes Miracle*. The victims of these mistakes in judgment quickly joined the alliance of the discontented.

Because of Tommy's spectacular early success, he saw no need to build alliances with networks of dedicated teachers or concerned parents in his school. He felt his involvement with the traditional parent–teacher organizations was enough. Consequently, he had no way of knowing just how much the ranks of the discontented had grown. He had no way of knowing that he was increasingly perceived as lacking empathy and being noncollaborative.

Eventually, Tommy expelled a student under the Zero Tolerance policy for bringing a dangerous weapon to school (a butter knife). The student had never been in trouble before. In the ensuing media uproar,

Tommy found he had no allies among the constituencies at the school. Dr. Spock, the superintendent, maintained a strictly objective, neutral stance while Tommy was hammered in the media for lacking empathy and concern for the youngsters in his care. Eventually, it was decided to move Tommy to the middle school as the assistant principal in charge of curriculum. Descartes's test scores continued to be among the highest in the school system.

The Prism of Emotion-based Interpersonal Skills

Point #1

People always view reality through their own emotional perspective. Although it was clear to Tommy and Dr. Spock that test scores were the main priority, the teachers of Descartes needed to be persuaded of that fact and then allowed to *buy into* the plan to raise test scores by participating in the development of the plan. The teachers never joined in the happiness of the success of Descartes because it was never part of the teachers' sense of owning part of the big picture at Descartes. Mr. Glick's plan and Dr. Spock's priorities had driven the process. The teachers, although an integral part of the process, viewed themselves as observers and not committed participants. The teachers' lack of commitment cost Tommy valuable allies.

Point #2

Listening is a key communication skill for leaders. It is very important to hear both what people say *and* what they mean. Your interpretation of what you hear can sometimes be fatal if it does not capture what people want you to hear.

Point #3

Networking is another key leadership skill (see Further Readings on Networking). It is a fundamental trait of humans to seek and trade information. Human survival depends on that information-seeking quality. Smart leaders tap into organizational information grapevines to see what is going on and how they are doing as leaders. It is unwise to ignore this seek-and-trade tendency in human nature and not be a part of informal networks and information grapevines.

Point #4

Research on the emotional make-up of men and women shows that people commit what behavioral and cognitive scientists call the fundamental attribution error. This is a tendency to believe that mistakes you make should be attributed to external factors but mistakes others make should be attributed to character flaws. If we are occasionally late for appointments, we may attribute our tardiness to traffic or some other factor outside our control. Those whom we keep waiting may attribute our lateness to a lack of concern about others. They may believe we do not have enough regard for them to be on time. Behavioral research indicates the human tendency to commit the fundamental attribution error occurs in many different settings and under many different circumstances. This is an important piece of research for leaders to consider.

What Tommy Could Have Done

If Tommy Glick had been aware of the latest information about emotions and human nature, he might have taken some or all of the following steps:

Step #1

Tommy could have identified teacher-leaders and nonteaching staff who could exercise leadership at Descartes Elementary. Working with this group as the Core Leadership Team, Tommy could have employed his considerable powers of persuasion to convince this group that the school should focus on test scores in the coming school year. In turn, these core leaders would have used their leadership and persuasive skills to convince the rest of the staff of the importance of making the testing program a priority. If Tommy had used this approach, he could have been assured that many more of the faculty and staff would take ownership of the testing initiative. If Tommy had chosen to work with and through others in exercising leadership, he would have gotten more people involved and engaged, thus gaining both allies and a constituency that both understood and approved of his approach to the problem. He also would have gained a committed following rather than a group that was, at best, passive in their acceptance of his main leadership thrust. If the faculty and staff had been emotionally committed to the focus on the testing program, they would have shared a greater sense of accomplishment with the rise in test scores.

Step #2

If Tommy had known the importance of active listening, he might not have missed the important messages of both teachers and parents as they expressed concerns about an overemphasis on test taking. Leaders must realize that their positions of authority make it very difficult for subordinates to express concerns and to voice even the mildest criticisms. Often, dissatisfaction will be stated in indirect or muted terms if expressed at all. In Tommy's case, teachers were reluctant to tell Tommy they believed there was too much emphasis on testing. Instead, they said things like "What do you think of this creative writing program? Do you see a place for it in our curriculum, consistent with the test preparation program?" Or they said, "Everything is going great in my classroom. I just wish I had a little more time for some different activities." Tommy could not hear what the teachers wanted him to hear. He only heard the surface message. Leaders with well-developed interpersonal skills, particularly active listening skills, are able to probe beneath the surface message and hear the buried communication that is so important to the survival and success of school leaders in a highly volatile period of school leadership. If Tommy had taken the step of listening actively for the underlying message, he would have known that a midcourse correction was needed in his leadership direction. Another look at the emphasis on testing was in order and a modification in the testing program was required.

Step #3

In addition to hearing and understanding the underlying message, modern-day school leaders know the importance of establishing and tapping into information networks. If Tommy Glick had taken the step to nourish communication grapevines both inside and outside of Descartes Elementary School, he would have known of the unhappiness with his leadership. Research shows successful leaders in many different arenas, including business, government, and the arts, spend substantial amounts of time cultivating contacts that can provide them with up-to-the-minute intelligence about what is happening both in their immediate environment and in the larger world of which they are a part. Tommy Glick should have taken the step of establishing networks of colleagues both in and outside of his building in the school system and community. This network could have alerted him to how he was being perceived. Information grapevines are as old as humankind, and as long as human beings require information for survival and success, information grapevines will be a major part of leadership.

Step #4

If Tommy Glick had been aware of the concept of the fundamental attribution error, he would have realized that his faculty tended to blame his occasional misstep on a deficiency in his character while he saw his mistakes as merely unavoidable circumstances. Tommy would have known that a stereotype of his character was being constructed in the minds of his faculty and he could have taken steps to correct that stereotype. Once again, a lack of knowledge about fundamental traits of human nature had unhappy consequences for a modern-day leader.

EMOTIONAL INTELLIGENCE (EQ)

The concept of emotional intelligence (EQ) gives us a handy term to describe the basis for many of the interpersonal skills we will be examining. Peter Salovey, a Yale psychologist, and John Mayer, who teaches psychology at the University of New Hampshire, developed the concept of emotional intelligence a decade ago. As scientists, their initial definition of the concept was very specific. They defined emotional intelligence as:

1. *Knowing one's emotions.* This is the skill of being able to identify with precision what you are feeling—knowing whether the emotion you are feeling is fear or anger, for example.

2. *Managing emotions.* This is the skill of using your emotions in a productive manner and not allowing your emotions to overwhelm you.
3. *Motivating oneself.* This is the ability to use your emotions to self-motivate.
4. *Recognizing emotions in others.* This is the ability to empathize, the skill of being able to put yourself in someone else's shoes.
5. *Handling relationships.* This skill includes the ability to recognize emotions in those around us and the ability to deal with others' emotions in productive ways.

As various authors have adopted the concept of emotional intelligence for their own uses and misuses, Salovey and Mayer found it necessary to revise their initial definition of EQ and have attempted to depict the precise nature of EQ with even greater exactitude. For our purpose of introducing the concept, however, the original definition will suffice.

Daniel Goleman, in his 1995 book *Emotional Intelligence*, popularized the concept of EQ. Since Goleman's book rose to the top of the bestseller lists, EQ has become part of the lexicon of our popular culture. Emotional intelligence has been cited as the most important factor in successful marriages, effective child rearing, winning career management, and productive homemaking. In fact, the concept is in danger of being used as a panacea for almost every imaginable problem. But it is important to remember that the notion of EQ is supported by more than eighty years of rigorous empirical research on the role and function of the emotions in decision making (see Further Readings on Emotional Intelligence). Although the term *emotional intelligence* may now be overused or misapplied to various human endeavors, the concept of EQ can provide powerful insights into human behavior and help school leaders both understand and predict the actions of people in organizations when used with precision and care. For example, teaming is a major factor in present-day school leadership. However, there is research that many teams are not effective (see Further Readings on Teaming). A fundamental problem encountered in teaming is negative interpersonal relationships among team members. Effective team members must be able to engage each other in open and vigorous disagreements without offending or creating long-lasting antagonisms. If team members are not candid and honest, then the productivity of the overall team is limited. Unfortunately candor and honesty can sometimes lead to negative feelings within the team. Cooper and Sawaf (1997) describe efforts to promote positive interpersonal relationships among team members by pinpointing the dialogue interruption patterns of individual team members and using this self-awareness to avoid emotional flash points in fellow team members. If the team leader can help the team members specify their precise emotional vulnerabilities and make team members aware of both their own and others' emotional sensitivities, group cohesion is enhanced and team effectiveness is increased. Therefore, raising the emotional intelligence of the team has a direct and positive impact on the team's productivity.

Persuasion is another key interpersonal skill based in emotional awareness. Early writers on leadership believed persuasion was needed only when leaders worked with those in or outside the organization who had greater or equal power to them. It was not necessary for leaders to practice persuasion on subordinates. Subordinates supposedly responded to directives from the top without additional motivation or emotional inducement. Modern school leaders know this is an outdated belief. To obtain commitment and enthusiastic support for school initiatives, persuasion is a necessary part of effective leadership. Although rational explanation is part of any act of persuasion, powerful, compelling persuasion is based primarily on a strong emotional appeal. Facts presented without an emotional context rarely move people to action. Successful advertisers, lawyers, and politicians are strongly aware of the emotional basis of persuasion.

Other professionals heavily involved in people enterprises realize that emotion drives attention, which in turn links to prior emotional experience, which in turn moves us to emotionally connected action. This is the way the mind works. Those who are attempting to persuade and lead people cannot ignore this neurological pattern.

Leadership, writes Gardner (1995), takes place in the minds of leaders and followers. Effective leaders tell stories with which followers can identify. These stories always contain the same essential elements. The stories tell the followers who they are, where they come from, and where they are going. If the stories are to motivate and inspire the followers, they must appeal as much to the followers' emotions as their intellects. Consequently, smart principals give a sense of identity and purpose to the teachers in their building by describing the teachers' efforts in the larger context of the teachers' constant struggle to improve and uplift humankind with nothing but the tools of their mind and their good intentions. Principals should emphasize that, despite immediate annoyances and irritations from overzealous accountability systems or well-meaning but difficult parents, teachers are always the good guys. In the final analysis, the health and stability of society rests upon those who teach. Teachers have the most important job in the world.

A LOOK AHEAD

The following chapters of this book examine the leadership tools of teaming and persuasion in more depth. We also scrutinize many other interpersonal skills reliant upon emotional knowledge and skills. Throughout this investigation, our basic premises remain constant. They are:

1. Working successfully with people is the one essential element for successful school leadership.
2. People are basically driven and motivated by their emotions. The intellect cannot make one feel and therefore cannot make one act.
3. New knowledge about the emotions must be incorporated into the exercise of leadership.

SUMMARY

New information and research as to how and why people think and behave as they do are still in the early stages of development. Greater understanding and enhanced ability to understand and predict human behavior is inevitable. Biological science has been incorporated into the art of medical healing only in the last 150 years. Today, medical treatment uninformed by biology is inconceivable. Soon, school leadership uninformed by the latest neurological information will seem equally unthinkable.

Neurological research, even in its infancy, is often complex and difficult to understand. Still, school leaders must grapple with this new information. They cannot ignore new findings or wait until the knowledge is presented in a more cogent and easily understood format. Information specialists say we are increasingly becoming two populations: those who understand the complex accoutrements of the modern world and those who do not. How many of us really comprehend the complex workings of the Internet or the mystical interplay of global financial markets? Even more complex and mystical are the inner workings of the human mind, an unexplored frontier of human knowledge. School leaders cannot afford to be among the unknowing in this vital area. If we ignore findings about how the mind works, we are as derelict as if we had ignored the latest findings about learning and curriculum.

We strive throughout this book to explain the latest research in the most straightforward manner possible. We attempt to use Ockham's razor as we proceed. Ockham was a thirteenth-century scientist who contended that the simplest explanation for phenomena was usually the most accurate account of those phenomena. We use Ockham's razor as we apply behavioral and neurological research to essential leadership skills. Let us begin.

FIVE FAST FUNDAMENTALS FROM THIS CHAPTER

1. The essence of leadership is people.
2. Human nature has not changed but we know more about it than ever.
3. We are fundamentally emotional, not rational, creatures.
4. Emotional intelligence is a prerequisite for effective leadership.
5. Communication is a key leadership skill and listening is the key to communication.

CHAPTER 2

What Leadership Is All About: The ABCs of Leadership

Because the primary focus for school leadership is working effectively with and through people, we would like to take you on a short tour of leadership thinking so that you will understand how it has evolved and how many of the things you already know connect with our view of leadership. Most important, we show you how you can use some old tools in combination with some new tools to become a more effective school leader.

What does it take to be a successful leader? If a leader is successful in one situation, will she be successful in all others? What do successful leaders know and do that less successful leaders do not know and/or cannot do? These questions have been asked throughout most of recorded history. This chapter examines the leadership thinking that is the foundation for a new approach to leadership with emotional intelligence at its center. We begin by looking at ideas about the nature of leadership that cut across all of its applications because there are key elements in all leadership situations that must be addressed by all leaders. Effective leadership, wherever and whenever it is found, is based on the application of three key elements and grounded in emotional intelligence. This chapter also focuses on the evolution in thinking about school leadership and the application of the key elements in the school setting. Through this review, we show how we developed our approach to leadership and how it is connected to emotional intelligence. To move forward, we must fully understand where we have been and where we are if we hope to clearly see where we need to go.

PRINCIPLES OF LEADERSHIP

So You Think You Learned to be a Leader in Graduate School

Bill, a recent graduate of the state university's principal preparation program and a new principal, found the study of leadership fascinating and wrote several papers on the application of leadership theory in the school setting. As a student, he often thought about how valuable his knowledge of leadership would be when he became a principal. As a first-year principal, Bill made a valiant effort to use the things he had learned about leadership to do a better job. Occasionally, he felt that his study of leadership helped him better understand the situations he faced, but this occurred less and less frequently as the pressures and demands of his job increased. Eventually, Bill found that the hectic pace of his job prevented him from even thinking about the things he had learned. When the university sent a survey asking for feedback on its leadership development program, Bill reported the program lacked the practical training needed to run a school. He suggested that the university reduce the time spent on leadership theory and spend more time on topics such as how to handle conflict, raise student test scores, and deal with parents.

Bill is typical of many graduates of principal preparation programs. When asked about their preparation, principals often report they learned to be school leaders on the job. Even professors who have returned to the principal's office report that they don't actually use very much of what they themselves teach. What does this mean to the school leaders who are facing pressures to change schools, improve test scores, make their schools safer, and keep parents happy? Are there any answers for the school leader who asks, "How can I be a more effective leader?"

This is a difficult question. Many school leaders find themselves in situations similar to Bill's. They thought they had learned to be a leader only to find running a school did not fit nicely into any of the theories they learned. Unfortunately, many school leaders become disillusioned with the idea they can learn anything useful from leadership research and new thinking about leadership. They often enroll in the University of Experience and try to learn what they can from their own successes and failures. Their hope is to make it to retirement without getting fired or becoming so frustrated with their jobs they have to leave the profession.

It is for this group of hard-working, frustrated school leaders and new school leaders like Bill that we are writing this book. We are former school leaders who have faced those same frustrations and have been tempted to give up any hope of learning something about leadership that will help us be more effective. We believe that there are answers to the questions school leaders ask about how to be more effective and that the answers can be found through a careful analysis of what we know about leadership and emotional intelligence. We do not add yet another leadership theory to the long list of theories already claiming to be *the* answer for those who want to be more effective leaders. Instead, we help you better understand how you can take control of your own development and become a more effective school leader.

What Have We Learned about Leadership

Throughout much of history, leadership roles were reserved for those born into ruling families. We call attention to this fact only to note that the study of leadership began at a time when leaders were thought to be omnipotent and omniscient. So why would ancient leaders be concerned with learning anything about leadership? History shows us that ancient rulers who possessed powers far in excess of any powers modern leaders command still failed. The reason they failed was often tied to their inability to gain the acceptance of their followers. One of leadership's most famous pieces of literature is Machiavelli's *The Prince*. It is a book in which Machiavelli advises his protégé, the prince, that he would *always need the favor of the inhabitants*. The importance of gaining the support and acceptance of followers was understood early in the study of leadership. A review of leadership literature shows that followers have been the basis for many leadership theories. Leadership literature is filled with theories that advise leaders on how to use motivation, power, and influence to be more effective.

As views on leadership have evolved, followers have become increasingly more important and diverse. In today's team-oriented society, followers are actually more like constituents than followers in the ancient sense. Therefore, we use the term *constituents* in this book to refer to those with whom leaders work and influence.

Key Principle One: The Importance of Constituents

From the volumes of print on the topic, it is logical to assume that scholars must know a great deal about leadership. We know more now than we have ever known, but we have yet to discover the ultimate formula for effective leadership and probably never will. All the theories about how leaders use power, influence, and motivation are flawed. The most valuable thing we know about leadership is that no single theory or approach will work in all situations. The complexities of human behavior will not allow it. As we stated in chapter 1, we believe leadership in schools is essentially working with people in a productive capacity. If you accept our premise, the difficulty of describing effective leadership qualities is evident. Human behavior is the most complex phenomenon on Earth and presents multiple, complex problems for leaders. Yet all leaders must reach their goals or their organization's goals through the work of others.

The main element of our first key leadership principle is:

- Consider Your Constituents

Few would argue that leadership theorists have been unsuccessful in answering their most important question, "What qualities make a leader effective?" Their work has, however, brought us to our present level of understanding. We are currently in the position in which Thomas Edison found himself as he searched for the ideal light bulb filament. We know a lot about what will not work and we know some things that do. We know that followers or constituents are key ingredients in a leader's success. We know many things about how power, influence, and motivation influence constituents, but we do not know how these and other factors affect specific leadership situations. We call your attention to the need to understand constituents within your context. The research and writing that has been done in this area will be useful, but you must apply the understanding of constituents and how they behave through the lens of your organization. In doing so, you use what you know without becoming entangled in theories that do not work in all situations. In later chapters, we add emotional intelligence as another lens through which constituents should be viewed.

Key Principle Two: The Situation

Leadership, as a concept, has taken on mythical qualities. In a world filled with uncertainty, we look to our leaders for order and predictability. If an organization is not succeeding, the leader is first held accountable. A recent newspaper article about a professional football coach illustrates this point and reveals some additional realities about the nature of leadership.

As the newly hired coach of the local professional football team, the coach faced a young reporter who asked what he would do to improve the team. The coach explained that he intended to continue to do the same things he had done in his former position as coach of an unsuccessful team in another city. In describing what he had done, he noted that he had carefully drafted players who would strengthen the team at key positions. He described a practice regimen that was grounded in sound physiological research and similar to the regimen used by the team that had last won the Super Bowl. He talked about the very competent coaching staff he had assembled. He then shifted his focus to the things that had happened to him and the team in his last year. Their top two draft picks had been injured in preseason games and had never recovered. Three of the team's top veterans had left the team over contract disputes. The offensive coordinator had struggled with the serious illness of his son throughout the season. He concluded his comments by reiterating that he would do the same things he had always done to lead his new team to success.

This account illustrates some important aspects of leadership. First, leaders are expected to be successful and they pay a price for failure. Second, leaders often do not or cannot change when they change leadership positions. They often use the same skills and knowledge in new situations. Third, all leaders face events over which they have little, or no, control.

What does this account teach us about leadership? It should come as no surprise to anyone that leaders are expected to succeed. Because some leaders appear to be able to effectively lead in difficult times and to be able to snatch victory from the jaws of defeat, we expect all our leaders to succeed. We have a selective memory when we recount the exploits of some of our great leaders. We choose not to talk about the Winston Churchill who could not retain the approval of his countrymen after World War II and was not reelected. We easily forgive the darker side of George Patton and forget that he could not function effectively as a leader when the hostilities ended. We want to believe that leaders always know what to do and how to do it. Our need for order and certainty requires nothing less. Equally unremarkable is the realization that leaders use what they know. How could they do otherwise?

In the newspaper article, the coach described his preparation for the coming season. That preparation was based on reasonable assumptions about the team's situation. In this case, the situation changed far more than he had anticipated and was a primary cause of his failure. The injuries, contract problems, and illness were out of his control. This situation, more than the coach's skill or his planning, dictated the team's fate. You may be thinking that it is a leader's ability to deal with the unexpected that defines effectiveness. If you do, it does not change the fact that the situation in which a leader functions is another key element of leadership.

The main element of our second key leadership principle is:

- Consider the Situation

One of the most interesting theories to come out of the situational approach to leadership is the theory developed by Robert Blake and Jane Mouton (1964). Their approach is grounded in a leader's sometimes conflicting need to attend to production (the output of the organization) and people (the constituents who actually produce the output). They developed the managerial grid in which the X-axis represents the leader's concern for production and the Y-axis represents the leader's concern for people. The grid is a tool leaders can use to determine their style.

When applied to the account of the new head coach's dilemma, the grid might have helped the coach define the changes he needed to make in his approach to the team and his staff. He might find it necessary to be more commanding with his team because of the loss of the veteran players. He might decide to be more sensitive with his assistant coach because of his son's illness and to be more direct with players and other coaches to compensate for his assistant's lack of focus on team issues.

Applied to school leadership, the grid can help a school leader analyze the situation and determine how to best use available time. For example, school leaders who find themselves in schools staffed with a large number of beginning teachers might use the grid to determine that both production (how to increase student achievement, manage classes better, etc.) and people (concern about feelings, needs, and problems) should both be high priorities. On the other hand, a principal who works with an experienced, self-directed staff might use the grid to determine that he should be more supportive than directive.

Regardless of how it is used, the managerial grid does not answer all the important questions about how best to lead. We discuss it here to show how it can be helpful as a tool. Other tools fall into the same category as the managerial grid. The list of further readings includes other resources that might be of interest to you. We encourage you to seek out other ideas and tools to use in the approach to professional growth (later in this chapter).

Key Principle Three: Every Leader Is an Individual

One of the things noted about the coach in the newspaper article was that he planned to use the knowledge and skills he had used in coaching his former team. Some organizations have tried to guarantee success by hiring a leader who has a proven success record. This strategy is not always successful. Another approach that has received attention in the leadership literature is commonly known as *trait theory* (see P. Northouse in Further Readings on Leadership Development). This approach to discovering the essence of effective leadership is based on the premise that all effective leaders possess certain skills, knowledge, and attitudes. If those qualities could be identified and taught, leadership success would be assured. Trait theory has contributed much to our knowledge of leadership, but has not been successful in identifying qualities that ensure a leader's success. It has, however, helped us identify our third and final key principle.

The main element of our third key leadership principle is:

- Consider Yourself

Effective leaders know themselves. They understand their strengths and weaknesses. They use this knowledge to be more effective by finding ways to compensate for their weaknesses through delegation, working to strengthen skills, and exercising extra caution when dealing with issues outside their competence. The search for self-understanding is a lifelong journey. It requires a willingness to learn from failures and successes. Often leaders assume that the world (their constituents and others) perceives them as they perceive themselves. Clearly, some leaders do not know what they do not know. They continue to operate in unproductive ways, oblivious to feedback and data. One of the most difficult things to know is how the world perceives us.

Leaders can increase their self-knowledge in a number of ways. One of the most useful is participation in a leadership assessment center. Other self-knowledge tools provide information about a leader's style or preferences. One of the most widely used tools is the Myers-Briggs Type Indicator. This indicator is based on Carl Jung's descriptions of psychological types. This instrument provides feedback on how individuals perceive and judge the world around them. Other tools that can provide important self-knowledge include 360-degree surveys that allow a leader to test self-perceptions against those of constituents and reflections on daily events in a leader's life (see *The Collaborative Professional Development Process* in Further Readings on Leadership Development).

In *Leadership: Theory and Practice*, Peter Northouse (2001) presents a thorough analysis of leadership theory. He notes that there are as many definitions of leadership and leadership theories as there are people who have studied and tried to define them. However, careful analysis of this confusing mass of theories and definitions reveals some essential pieces of the leadership development puzzle. We have already noted that our view of leadership includes the leadership situation, the constituents, and the unique mix of skills, beliefs, knowledge, and experiences a leader brings to the situation. Recent discoveries about how emotions affect human behavior have added greatly to our understanding of leadership. This book is about how leaders can increase their effectiveness by considering their situations, their constituents, and themselves through the microscope of emotional intelligence. In figure 2.1, this approach is graphically displayed.

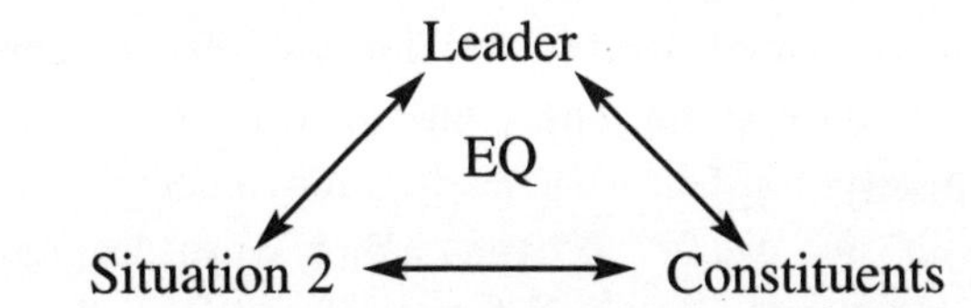

Figure 2.1. *Key Principles for Developing Your Individualized Plan*

So What?

So what can this new view of leadership do to help you learn to be a more effective leader? How is this different from what Bill found so interesting in graduate school, but what he found to be only occasionally helpful in the real world of school leadership? We address both those questions by asking you to view our approach to leadership in a different way. Leaders are on a journey to find the knowledge and skills that will enable them to effectively lead their organizations. We would like you to view our key principles of leadership as travel aids for your journey. We see these keys as the pen, paper, and scale you need to draw a road map for your journey. Your map should show you the major roads, the secondary roads, and the dirt roads you will encounter. It should warn you about danger areas, hazards you will encounter, and help you avoid areas that will hinder or end your journey. You will need these tools to draw a map, but the map you draw is up to you. As with all maps, some are better than others. Your success in drawing your map will depend on many factors. Some of those factors are the additional tools we have noted that will help you understand constituents, situations, and yourself. The most important factor is you. It is your desire to be better that ultimately determines your success. The tools make the job easier, but you determine your success through your tenacity and determination in the face of resistance, stress, and pressure to produce.

Viewing leadership as a journey also implies a singular effort. That is how we see it. You will be making an individual journey as you strive to become a more effective leader. No one theory, set of skills, or learning will ensure your success as a leader. We think that your success is in your hands and that the situation in which you find yourself, your constituents, and the things you bring to the role will affect you in significant ways. We hope that making you aware of these factors and showing you how emotional intelligence affects each of them will enable you to develop you own leadership theory grounded in your situation, with your constituents, and connected to your individuality.

PRINCIPLES OF SCHOOL LEADERSHIP

Now that we have told you how we view leadership, you are probably wondering how our thinking relates to school leaders. When compared to the study of general leadership, school leadership is an infant. Many pre-1900s schools resembled the one-room schools depicted in popular television shows. School leadership consisted of managing a school as its lead teacher. Since its inception early in the last century, school leadership has reflected the general trends in business management. This certainly was true in the early 1900s. School administration was focused on finance, business management, physical equipment, and personnel management. Next, school administration researchers moved to the behavioral sciences, along with general leadership research, in their search for school leadership wisdom. This began the search for the perfect set of leader behaviors. The behavioral science era in school administration mirrored a similar movement in business management thinking. Many of the trait theories of leadership discussed earlier in this chapter evolved at this time. Currently, we are in the standards/accountability era of school administration. This era is marked by calls for school leaders to be instructional and change leaders in their schools. This era has also seen acceleration in the development of standards for students and other educators.

In the mid-1970s, the National Association of Secondary School Principals (NASSP) developed a set of skills that represented current thinking about what school leaders should be able to do. This list of skills became the basis for the association's assessment center that was designed to identify the strengths and weaknesses in candidates interested in school leadership. Armed with the report that was generated by this assessment, a superintendent could choose the candidate best suited for any given school opening. The NASSP never claimed that their skills were inclusive of all the requirements of effective school leadership, but this assessment was the only source of data available to superintendents who wanted to choose wisely from the large pool of available candidates and was widely used. Several states even used the assessment to make administrative licensure decisions. We address these skills again in chapter 4.

As calls for more emphasis on student achievement and instructional leadership increased, critics called for new thinking on school leadership and a shift away from the management approach reflected in the NASSP skills. In the early 1990s, the National Policy Board for Educational Administration (NPBEA), a consortium of ten national school administration-related organizations, took on the task. The result was the NPBEA 21 Domains. The 21 Domains are revisited in chapter 4.

In 1995, *The Knowledge Base in Educational Administration: Multiple Perspectives* was published. Some of the leading researchers and authors in school leadership used this publication to attack the NPBEA domains on a variety of grounds. This book (see Further Readings on Leadership Development) claims that the diverse voices of race, ethnicity, and gender have been excluded from the thinking and research that informed the domains. The ability to define school leadership using the behavioral sciences approach was also challenged. The editors point out in their introduction that "What we know always has something to do with who we are, where we have been, who has socialized us, and what we believe."

The most recent attempt to define the qualities essential for effective school leadership is embodied in the Interstate School Leaders Licensure Consortium (ISLLC) Standards. These six standards and their accompanying knowledge, disposition, and performance indicators represent the first set of national standards for school leaders. The ISLLC Standards were used to develop a licensure assessment for school leaders currently being used by several states and the District of Columbia. This latest attempt to define the knowledge base for school leadership has intensified the controversy over the exact nature of effective school leadership.

The Interstate School Leaders Licensure Consortium Standards

Standard 1

A school administrator is an educational leader who promotes the success of all students by facilitating the development, articulation, implementation, and stewardship of a vision of learning that is shared and supported by the school community.

Standard 2

A school administrator is an educational leader who promotes the success of all students by advocating, nurturing, and sustaining a school culture and instructional program conducive to student learning and staff professional growth.

Standard 3

A school administrator is an educational leader who promotes the success of all students by ensuring management of the organization, operations, and resources for a safe, efficient, and effective learning environment.

Standard 4

A school administrator is an educational leader who promotes the success of all students by collaborating with families and community members, responding to diverse community interests and needs, and mobilizing community resources.

Standard 5

A school administrator is an educational leader who promotes the success of all students by acting with integrity, fairness, and in an ethical manner.

Standard 6

A school administrator is an educational leader who promotes the success of all students by understanding, responding to, and influencing the larger political, social, economic, legal, and cultural context.

There is little agreement about the qualities that ensure effective school leadership. For example, the ISLLC Standards were developed through the participation of thirty-seven states, yet many of those states elected to develop their own state standards even though they grant an administrative license based on an assessment based on the national standards. The standards (both national and state) do little to help school leaders build the knowledge and skills needed to meet these standards. Standards are written in outcome language. By that, we mean they tell you what you need to be or achieve. They say nothing about what you should do to accomplish those outcomes. We want to show you how you can become a more effective leader through emotional intelligence's impact on the analysis of situations, constituents, and self.

USING EMOTIONAL INTELLIGENCE AND THE LEADERSHIP KEYS TO IMPROVE

We hope that this book will encourage you to use our ideas to improve your leadership capabilities. If you are to do that, you need a method that will work. We believe that your professional development should be under your control. We have suggested an overall approach to leadership development and we address the application of that approach to specific situations administrators encounter (in later chapters). If you are to fully utilize this information, you have to plan your development.

You will see the *Handbook of Leadership Development* and the *Lessons of Experience* listed in the Further Readings on Leadership Development. These two books from the Center for Creative Leadership give you a more detailed view of the strategy we are suggesting you incorporate as you use our approach.

Your development is an individual journey. You will find many tools helpful as you work to better understand the situations you encounter, the constituents with whom you work, and the things you bring with you as the leader. None of these tools are complete in and of themselves. You must take ownership of and responsibility for your development. That does not mean you should not ask for help or even demand it. It does mean that you are the only one who can solve the equation that the key leadership components and emotional intelligence create in the atmosphere in which you work.

So how should you proceed? First, you need to understand few things. When you are working to improve your leadership effectiveness, you should expect the following:

- You will probably feel less comfortable when you try new, more effective behaviors than when you use old, less effective behaviors.

- When you try something new, things will most likely get worse before they get better. (This is known as the implementation dip.)
- Your colleagues will probably not understand your new behaviors. (It is a good idea, therefore, to let them in on what you are doing.)
- Change takes time. Be patient with your team, your organization, and yourself.
- You will need to constantly evaluate, assess, and work to better understand yourself, the others with whom you work, and the situation in which you are functioning.

Our key elements define the guideposts for your development, and the application of emotional intelligence will help you be more effective. Alone, however, this is not enough. You must use the laboratory in which you work to conduct the experiments that will help you discover the personal leadership style that will increase your effectiveness. That laboratory is full of danger. Your actions will be constantly evaluated and critiqued. But you must use your laboratory to learn how to better lead your school. It is through application that learning is meaningful. Unlike classroom or workshop learning, learning from experience sticks with you. So what are the key elements of learning from experience?

Learning from experience requires effort. It is more difficult to learn from an experience than to just get through it on your way to the next. Learning requires reflection on what happened, why it happened, what part you played in the success or failure of the event, the ability to be honest with yourself about what you did well and poorly, and the ability to apply the learning in future situations. Data and feedback are the road signs on your journey. Support from others willing to mentor, provide feedback, or provide other needs is important. The support of others will get you through the painful lessons and confirm your growth. It will be important to obtain the support of your boss. In the final analysis, however, you are in charge and it will be your motivation that will, to a great extent, determine your success.

It will be important for you to seek a variety of experiences and to seek challenging assignments. If your work does not challenge you, it will not provide learning opportunities. Seek to learn from others with whom you work. Learn from their effective and ineffective behaviors. Your goal in this is not to become like them or to copy their behaviors, but to truly learn more about situations or constituents. For example, you might watch a skilled leader engage constituents in decision making and learn more about how constituents react or more about the nature of situations in which decisions are made.

Learn from the conflict situations in which you find yourself. Conflict is generally not something leaders seek. It is, however, a necessary step to improvement. If there are no conflicts, there is no progress or improvement. Without conflict, we continue to do things the same way. Viewing conflict as productive and learning how to manage conflict by making it constructive rather than destructive are key leadership traits. School leadership provides many opportunities to deal with conflict; from this laboratory, many leadership lessons may be learned.

You might be thinking, "This sounds fine, but what am I supposed to do?" We cannot answer that question for you. You must answer it. We provide you with examples and tools in the chapters that follow, but you must take that knowledge and those tools and apply them in your unique situation. We think that demonstrating the importance of our three key components and helping you apply emotional intelligence as you analyze each of them will help you learn the things that will make you a better leader.

SUMMARY

Leadership effectiveness is determined by the interplay of the three key components all leaders face: constituents, situations, and leader self-knowledge. Constituents play a vital role in a leader's success. Leaders work through their constituents. The situations in which leaders function significantly influence their success. The ability to read situations and make any necessary adjustments is a vital leadership trait. Leaders themselves are factors in their success. An understanding of self is another must for effective leadership. The leadership literature is full of answers to the question, "What makes a great leader?" None of the answers have been complete, but they provide important insights into the nature of leadership. The research on leadership has resulted in the development of many tools that can help leaders better understand constituents, situations, and themselves.

Within education, efforts to describe the ideal school leader have been unsuccessful. The current set of national standards for school leaders focuses on the importance of instructional leadership, but does not address how the leaders obtain the outcomes they describe. In the final analysis, becoming a more effective leader is a never-ending journey that involves integration of the key components and emotional intelligence with a strong desire to improve. In the day-to-day world in which leaders function are laboratories in which leaders can learn how to be more effective through the individualized plans they develop.

FIVE FAST FUNDAMENTALS FROM THIS CHAPTER

1. The three key elements of leadership are the constituents, the situation, and the leader.
2. Consideration of these three elements can enhance the process of learning from experience in leadership.
3. Research on leadership can be helpful in developing leadership skills when used as part of an overall program of reflection and practice.
4. Good leaders learn as much from failure as success.
5. Leadership development requires patience and the help of constituents throughout the organization.

CHAPTER 3

Emotion-Based Interpersonal Skills

In chapter 2, we described three principle considerations for leadership: constituents, the situation, and you, the leader. This chapter covers each of these primary components of leadership through the lens of emotion-based interpersonal skills. Again, our basic premises are:

1. Working successfully with people is essential for effective leadership.
2. People are driven by their emotions. The intellect cannot make one feel and therefore cannot make one act.
3. New knowledge about the emotions must be understood and used by school leaders.

A brief vignette will illustrate the interaction of the three components of leadership and the emotions.

A DIFFICULT MEETING

Ms. Lexus, principal of Main Street Middle School, is about to begin an important meeting. The meeting is with the seventh-grade math teacher, Mr. Stone. Mr. Stone is knowledgeable about mathematics. In fact, Mr. Stone has an excellent grasp of math content from Algebra I through Calculus II. Although well informed about mathematics, Mr. Stone has difficulty adapting his classroom curriculum to the knowledge level of his students. He once stated to his fellow seventh-grade team members, "I teach math, not students." In addition to his classroom problems, Mr. Stone does not get along well with students, fellow teachers, or parents. Mr. Stone has expressed an interest in transferring to the high school. Unfortunately, his lack of social skills has hindered the transfer.

Preparing for the Meeting: Assessing the Leader's Emotions

Ms. Lexus should carefully monitor and regulate her feelings before, during, and after the meeting. She should ask herself a series of questions about the encounter with Mr. Stone. Does Mr. Stone's behavior trigger anger in Ms. Lexus because of what she believes to be his refusal to meet the needs of his students? Is her strongest feeling anxiety, or even fear, that the meeting may result in a grievance, or some other action against her, by Mr. Stone? Is Ms. Lexus emotionally exhausted by continuing difficulties with Mr. Stone? Prior to the meeting, Ms. Lexus should determine her dominant feelings. Until she identifies her emotions, she cannot successfully control them.

Regulating the Leader's Emotions

Different feelings call for different self-regulation methods. If Ms. Lexus is angry, she could try to view Mr. Stone's behavior from Mr. Stone's viewpoint. Mr. Stone probably does not want to impede student learning. He probably believes that in the long run his teaching methods are the best way for most students to learn or Mr. Stone simply may not know another way to teach. Ms. Lexus needs to put herself in Mr. Stone's shoes to see the situation from his perspective. Empathizing with Mr. Stone's view should alleviate Ms. Lexus's anger. If Ms. Lexus fears problems with Mr. Stone after the meeting, she can confront that fear by imagining a best-case scenario (Mr. Stone is satisfied with the meeting) to a worst-case scenario (Mr. Stone files a grievance). Ms. Lexus should then conduct the meeting in such a way that a grievance, if filed, is unjustified. Finally, if Ms. Lexus is emotionally exhausted, she should acknowledge the stress and incorporate stress-reducing activities into her life. Whatever her approach, Ms. Lexus must first assess her feelings before she can take appropriate action.

Assessing the Constituent's Emotions

In addition to being sensitive to her own emotions, Ms. Lexus must be sensitive to Mr. Stone's emotional state. Is Mr. Stone angry because of his inability to transfer to the high school? Is a fear of failure as a teacher driving Mr. Stone's behavior? Ms. Lexus's analysis of Mr. Stone's emotions can determine how Ms. Lexus facilitates her encounter with Mr. Stone.

Acknowledging Emotional Parameters of a Situation

In order to ascertain Mr. Stone's basic motivation, Ms. Lexus needs to ask questions and employ the most important of communication skills: listening. Research indicates that questioning is a less threatening form of communication than assertion. By questioning and active listening, Ms. Lexus can channel this encounter into a more flexible and productive area of discussion than the traditional difficult teacher-principal encounter. If Ms. Lexus uses these interpersonal skills, the meeting can have a different tone and move in a different direction. In the usual teacher-with-problems and principal conference, the principal begins the meeting by stating what she sees as the problem, or stating the specific incident that triggered the meeting, and asking the teacher to respond. Underlying this exchange will be strong emotions on the part of both participants. These emotions are rarely acknowledged and even less frequently dealt with. By acknowledging that this situation is fraught with strong emotional overtones, analyzing her own emotions, drawing from Mr. Stone's responses about how he perceives the situation, and then working through Mr. Stone's anger or fear, Ms. Lexus can work in a productive manner with Mr. Stone, as opposed to allowing emotions on both sides to become an obstruction. To paraphrase a line from Arthur Miller's play *Death of a Salesman*, emotions are something to which attention must be paid.

In the preceding vignette, we analyzed the leader, constituents, and the situation through the prism of emotional intelligence. We studied a specific situation and applied research on the emotions to leadership behavior and the leader's interaction with a constituent. In the remainder of this chapter, we investigate emotion-based interpersonal skills as they apply to constituents in the selection of personnel, communication and persuasion, and team building. We also assess the emotional parameters of leadership situations.

INTERPERSONAL SKILLS

Selection of Personnel

The reality of leadership is that difficult encounters with constituents are always a possibility. However, research has been conducted on interpersonal skills and traits conducive to success in the workplace. These personality dimensions can help create good personal relations in the work environment and are found to lead to more effective performance. This research has the potential to assist school leaders in the selection and hiring of personnel. Baron (1996), after reviewing the research on personality dimensions associated with success in the workplace, lists five personal qualities of interest to leaders.

1. Extraversion: The ability to be sociable and active in relations with others.
2. Agreeableness: The ability to cooperate as well as forgive apparent offenses.
3. Conscientiousness: The ability to apply self-discipline and organization to a task.
4. Emotional Stability: The ability to maintain emotional security in changing and challenging circumstances.
5. Openness to Experience: The ability to demonstrate sensitivity to others and the environment.

The research on personality dimensions associated with success in the workplace, like much investigation of interpersonal skills, is still in its early stage. Personnel who are predisposed to good interpersonal relations can minimize the frequency of difficult encounters with constituents and the principal. School leaders should use this information in the selection process when possible and be aware of ongoing research developments in this area.

Few leaders have the freedom to personally select all of the people with whom they will work. The research on personnel selection is not infallible. Because limitations in personnel selection are a fact of leadership, it is also important to use other research that will help the leader understand and predict the behavior of the people with whom he works. Effective leaders have long known it is important to know your constituents. Recent research about how people process information can provide a specific focus and context for knowledge about constituents.

Senge (1999) asserts that the essence of leadership is communication. In fact, he contends that 98 percent of a leader's time is devoted to some form of communication. The work life of principals and superintendents is driven by communication. The lifeblood of the public school leader is face-to-face communication with constituents in which the school leader employs active listening skills and persuasion in encounters with teachers, students, parents, and other members of the school community.

Despite the emphasis in graduate schools of education on written communication, the reality of school leadership is that a principal or superintendent's day is a series of brief, verbal encounters broken by longer meetings and an occasional solitary session to do paperwork and dash off memos. A great deal of literature exists about leadership communication. Little of that literature speaks about the constituents receiving the communication. Research on how people process information can be used to enhance communication between leaders and constituents.

People process information in different ways. Awareness of how constituents handle the information you communicate can help the leader tailor her message so that the possibility of an effective communication exchange is increased and persuasion occurs. Summarizing the research on information processing, Chaiken, Gruenfeld, and Judd (2000) describe the different modes of information processing as heuristic and systematic.

Heuristic Information Processing

Those who process information in a heuristic manner focus on a few broad features of the subject under consideration. Examples of items on which they might focus are credibility of the source of the information and how many people agree about a particular aspect of the subject. A heuristic processor, when presented with a new instructional technique, will probably want to know if anyone he knows has successfully used the technique or, even more importantly, if anyone he knows has failed while using the technique. The heuristic processor will turn off when presented with a wealth of details about the initiative. Let's call these people the *big picture guys*.

Systematic Information Processing

Systematic information processing is characterized by a more rigorous, careful analysis of the details of the issue being scrutinized. Close scrutiny of many aspects of the subject being studied is a hallmark of systematic information processing. A systematic processor will want to know the details of any instructional technique with which he is presented. For example, he may want to analyze each step of the instructional technique. Let's call these folks the *detail guys*. Note that neither form of information processing is judged more effective than the other form. Although the heuristic mode can lead to superficial judgments, systematic processing sometimes leads to *paralysis through analysis*.

Implications for Leadership Communication and Persuasion

A need for flexibility in communicating with constituents is the main lesson to be learned by studying the research on information processing. Some constituents will want details about a change initiative. By questioning and by using active listening skills, the leader can ascertain which constituents want detailed, comprehensive information. The school leader can then supplement his face-to-face discussion with these constituents by furnishing additional documents, books, and so forth. If the school leader fails to follow up with more detailed information for these constituents, they might become frustrated and perhaps even hostile to the leader's initiative. They might even decide that the leader is attempting to cover up or stonewall factual information.

On the other hand, heuristic processors will not require detailed information. In fact, they might consider the presentation of extra documentation useless and an attempt to hide the real effects of an initiative. For the heuristic processor, the key communication skill is figuring out what important pieces of information he really needs in order to make up his mind. The leader can figure out what information the heuristic processor wants to process by asking him and listening carefully to his answer. Once again, active listening is essential.

The preceding discussion assumes an important point. Principals and superintendents, while exercising leadership through communication, must engage in a great deal of face-to-face persuasion. No major initiative should begin with the issuance of a position paper or other information document. The leader should begin any change initiative with face-to-face persuasion and information exchanges with key constituents. These sessions are in addition to the daily face-to-face encounters in which a leader taps into information networks and listens and persuades constituents. During these exchanges, leaders should consider the following basics of the art of communication described by Krauss and Morsella (2000):

1. *When persuading, be prepared to restate the same idea in various forms.* We perceive situations in different ways. When we state the same point in different ways, we increase the chances of connecting with the perceptions of the person with whom we are communicating.
2. *When listening, try to understand what the constituent intends to say.* Often, people do not say precisely what they mean. Active listening consists of using context clues and asking questions to pinpoint the message the person speaking to you wants to convey.
3. *Consider how the constituent will interpret what you say by considering the constituent's perspective.* An important part of communication is the ability to put yourself in the shoes of the people with whom you are communicating. If you can understand the perspective of the one receiving information, you can tailor the message for maximum effectiveness.
4. *Establish conditions of cooperation that enhance communication.* Communication does not take place in a vacuum. The actions of the leader before a particular communication effort and the actions of the leader after a specific communication shape how a person reacts to the information that is received. If the leader is sensitive to constituents, her communication will be received in

that light. If the leader tends to ignore the needs and views of people in the school or school system, that fact will influence how her communication is received.

5. *Consider message form.* How you communicate is sometimes almost as important as what you communicate. A quick, impersonal e-mail message would not be the way to communicate your serious displeasure with the performance of a subordinate. Face-to-face communication is always appreciated when important information needs to be exchanged. Some researchers contend that as much as 75 percent of any face-to-face exchange consists of nonverbal communication. When participants meet in the same room, both participants can observe body language and other nonverbal cues. Assessing nonverbal communication allows both participants to gauge the emotional state of the other person and more accurately assess the impact of the information exchanged. Although face-to-face communication requires more time and more planning than other methods of communication, this mode of communication pays off in more effective encounters with constituents. It's like the old automotive oil commercial used to say, "you can pay now or pay later" for ineffective communication and inappropriate modes of discourse.

Team Building and Constituents

Another important tool in the leaders' arsenal for working with constituents is the use of teams. The utilization of the team concept allows the leader to interact with diverse sets of constituents on issues of importance to the school community. The effective use of teams demands a high level of interpersonal and emotion-based skills (see Further Readings on Teaming). Employing the expertise of a group of constituents in a team allows the leader to apply expertise and experience to problems and needs that traditional organizational arrangements do not allow. For example, the use of a cross-disciplinary team to explore curriculum problems at the senior grade level of a high school can uncover gaps and overlaps in the curriculum not readily evident to the teachers organized by subject matter. The use of teams also fosters collegiality and democratic decision making and creates a more collaborative school culture. However, research indicates that many teams do not work well together and are not productive (Hackman 1990). A primary reason for the lack of productivity is that teams must go through a bonding or role adoption stage before they can begin to work together. If this stage is not successful, the team will not be productive (Hollenbeck, Lepine, and Ilgen 1996). Members must meet two criteria to become useful members of the team: (1) they must first possess some expertise needed by the team and (2) they must possess standing or status in the team so that other team members accept their expertise. If both conditions do not exist, they cannot serve the team productively. The possession of expertise by members of the team is not enough. They must also be able to share their expertise and accept the expertise of other team members.

The research on team building has several implications. First, teams should not be put together on a random basis. Team members should be selected for the expertise they possess to accomplish the mission. The leader does not do a constituent a favor if he selects that constituent for a team, but the constituent does not have information that is useful to the team. Second, leaders should realize teams must undergo a process of assimilation and learning how to work with each other. The leader can facilitate this process by modeling inclusive behavior for team members. He can call on various team members to present information in their areas of expertise and ensure that their input is recognized and valued or he can train those designated as team leaders in this team-building skill. Good teams do not happen by accident. They are the product of design, the application of interpersonal skills, and knowledge of the emotional glue that bonds an effective team together.

Assessing the Emotional Parameters of the Situation

An article in the October 26, 2000, issue of *USA Today* (Michaels 2000) illustrates the consequences of ignoring the emotional aspects of a transitional leadership situation. The article told the story of Norm Blake, who had resigned as chief executive officer of the U.S. Olympic Committee after serving for a period of eight months. Mr. Blake had successfully led U.S. Fidelity and Guaranty from the brink of bankruptcy and guided Promus Hotel Corporation to a successful merger with Hilton Hotels. Unfortunately, his attempt to change the structure and culture of the U.S. Olympic Committee headquarters was a different situation and called for different interpersonal skills. In summing up Blake's difficulties, *USA Today* writer Vicki Michaels commented, "The USOC knew it was getting a corporate guy in Blake, one who is much more accustomed to balancing ledger sheets that to balancing competing interests and human emotion" (Michaels 2000, 2c). The events related in *USA Today* are not uncommon in the leadership arena. Leaders must always be aware that any change raises strong emotions. Our first response to change is emotional. The reaction may be joy, anxiety, or fear. No matter what the reaction, school leaders must be cognizant of the effect emotion plays in any change process. As a new principal or superintendent, assessing the emotional baggage left in your leadership situation by your predecessor should be the first order of business. In working through any change initiative, assessing the emotional reactions of constituents is a high priority. We will grapple with this subject again in future chapters.

SUMMARY

In this chapter, we have looked at constituents, situations, and you, the leader, through the lens of emotion-based interpersonal skills. We reviewed strategies for assessing your emotions and the emotions of constituents prior to interactions in which conflicts are likely to arise. Research on interactions in the workplace was reviewed. School leaders often find themselves in situations in which conflicts can and do arise. Their communications skills are crucial to success in these situations. Understanding the communication process and how individuals process information is important for the leader. Research has shown that there are two modes of information processing: heuristic and systematic. Leaders must be flexible with their communication style in order to communicate effectively with constituents. The need for flexible communication styles is of particular importance as principals respond to calls to build teams within their schools.

FIVE FAST FUNDAMENTALS FROM THIS CHAPTER

1. Leaders must understand their own emotional make-up.
2. Leaders must understand the emotional make-up of their constituents.
3. Seventy-five percent of communication is about empathy.
4. Team leading and team building are no longer hit-or-miss propositions.
5. Leaders who ignore the emotional parameters of a situation can get hurt.

CHAPTER 4

The Nuts and Bolts of Leadership

Organizations that are being lead effectively function like well-oiled machines. Everyone in the organization seems to know what to do and how to do it. A sense of harmony and cooperation is evident. Problems are handled quickly and efficiently. When asked about their work, employees describe what they do in ways that make it sound more like a mission than a job. Some even say they would probably continue to do the work even if they were not paid (but quickly add, "Don't tell anyone!").

Effective schools are like other effective organizations in a number of ways. The most important similarity is leadership. No organization can be more effective than its leadership. In this chapter, we explore the relationship between effective schools and their equally effective leaders. As we do this, we continue to use emotional intelligence, constituents, and situations as the lens through which we view effectiveness, but we make leaders themselves our primary focus. We discuss the skills leaders use or fail to use that affect their effectiveness. We add skills to the list of tools available to school leaders who want to understand themselves better.

A GOOD FIRST IMPRESSION

Jane Jefferson has just been appointed principal of a new school in a new district. She is excited about this opportunity and understands the importance of getting off to a good start as she begins her new job. Because the new school will bring together teachers from several established schools in the district, Jane decides to invite the teachers to a special open house prior to the first teacher workday. She sits down at her computer and writes the following letter to the teachers assigned to the new school:

> Dear Faculty:
>
> I know you are as excited as I am about the coming year and our new school. In order for you to see our building and to answer some of your questions, I have decided to have a meeting prior to the first workday. This meeting is optional, but I am sure you will want to see the building and your classrooms. The meeting will also give us an opportunity to talk about how we are going to insure [*sic*] that our students are prepared for the new state test.
>
> Sincerely,
> Jane Jefferson
> Principal

Jane hopes her new faculty will view this letter in the following ways:

- My new principal is excited about the new school and the coming year. I will enjoy working with this energetic, motivated leader.
- How nice that the principal is going out of her way to plan a special meeting just for me so that I can see the new school and get my questions answered.
- The new principal is a true instructional leader. She is already thinking about how we can prepare for the new state test that has been on my mind since last year.
- I am really going to enjoy working in this school and with this principal who is already looking out for me.

A Teacher Reacts

When Tom Riddle gets Jane's letter, his reaction is not what Jane expects. Tom is a veteran teacher with only three years left until retirement. He takes pride in being perceived as a good teacher by his students and their parents. He is a bit strong willed and has had a few disagreements with his former principal. Tom figures that his name was put on the list for transfer to the new school because of those disagreements. He has, however, taken a philosophical approach to the transfer and, even though he would rather stay in his old school, he has decided to give the new school a try.

When Tom reads Jane's letter, he has the following reaction:

- This principal appears to be one of those eager new principals with little experience.
- He is annoyed by her assumption he is *excited* about being assigned to the school.
- He questions her common sense in assuming that he has not availed himself of the opportunity to tour the new school as it was being built. He is also annoyed about her lack of knowledge concerning his participation on the district planning team that developed the specifications for the building.
- He is angered by what he perceives as an order to be at this *optional* meeting unless he wants to be perceived as uncaring. Tom runs a lawn-mowing business in the summer to supplement his teaching salary and would not be able to attend even if he wanted to.
- He is most upset about the reference to testing. The state accountability movement has caused great stress and frustration in the district. Teachers are constantly being warned that they may lose their jobs if students do not perform on the state test. Now he assumes this new principal is going to get teachers to come to school early on the pretext of seeing the building only to beat them up on the testing issue again.
- As he puts the letter down, Tom reflects, "I thought I could live through this change at the end of my career. Perhaps I will reconsider."
- Last, he notices that Jane misspelled *ensure*. He wonders what kind of leader would send a letter with a spelling error to teachers she has never met.

The Impact of a Leader's Assumptions

It is clear from the reaction of this teacher that Jane already has a problem with Tom and other faculty who may react in a similar manner. This problem was caused by Jane's assumptions about the teachers and the situation. Jane did what she had done in her old job as an assistant principal in a district where she knew the situation and understood the constituents with whom she was working. Just as important, the constituents in her old district knew her. It is important to note that Jane wrote her letter with the intention of winning over the faculty with her enthusiasm and openness. This had worked well for her as an assistant principal because her principal was not comfortable with faculty and was very low energy. Jane had used her openness and energy to balance the principal's demeanor. As a result, she developed a high level of trust and cooperation with the faculty and the principal. The successes she had in this position were a major factor in the board's decision to offer her this principalship. So what happened?

Jane did not consider how best to work with faculty in this new setting. She assumed that what had worked previously would continue to work. She wrote a memorandum to the entire faculty and she did it without learning very much about her new constituents. For example, she did not know that many faculty members had visited the school as it was being built or that many had served on the building design team. She would have been well served by taking time to find out as much as she could about her new constituents before writing her letter. Certainly, Jane could not have learned all that she needed to know about her constituents prior to the beginning of the year, but she would have been well served if she had taken time to gather some information. You will recall that constituents are one of the key elements we identified in chapter 2. The situation Jane faced illustrates how important knowing your constituents can be.

From the skills perspective, Jane should have utilized problem analysis skills to find out as much as possible about her constituents. For example, she could have asked the district office how the new school was designed. She could have asked the teachers' former principals to share some insights about them and for suggestions on how to approach them. Another skill she could have used is judgment or decision making. Jane made some assumptions in her letter that were not supported by factual information. For example, she assumed that they would be happy about being assigned to the new school. A call to the personnel office could have clarified that assumption quickly. She also assumed that the comment about the state testing would be seen in a positive light, but she did not check on attitudes about testing.

Jane did not consider how the situation surrounding the new school would affect her communications. The stress that comes with change is well documented. For some, this stress is a motivator, as it was with Jane. For others, it is a major problem that must be addressed before progress can be made. This is the issue with Tom. He does not view moving to the new school as a good change. He needs to be reassured that he will be able to continue to work as effectively with his students and their parents as he did in his old school. He wants to work with a leader who will support him and be more open to his ideas than his previous principal had been. Tom is a good teacher who is feeling pressure because of the state's accountability system. Tom is the kind of teacher Jane needs to have on her team at the new school. Tom, however, is reconsidering whether he even wants to give the new school and new leader a chance. The situation in which Jane and Tom find themselves is having a significant impact on their attitudes and behaviors. As the leader, Jane is responsible for considering the situation. She should have used her problem analysis and judgment skills to find out more about the school's particular situation. She then could have adjusted her message to her constituents.

Ironically, Jane wants to be the kind of leader Tom wants her to be. Her lack of consideration of the situation Tom and his colleagues are facing has resulted in a critical misstep. Had Jane researched the issues facing the new school, she might have been able to address some of Tom's concerns, communicate openness to new ideas, and express a desire to work with the faculty in solving the problems they face.

Constituents Make Assumptions, Too

Tom used Jane's letter to form an initial impression about her leadership ability. In writing the letter, Jane thought she was effectively communicating her motivation and ability to lead the school. Jane was using the skills that had served her well in her previous job as an assistant principal in another district. She had written many similar letters and had gotten very positive feedback on her energy and positive attitude. She had also received praise for her focus on instructional issues and concern for students. This feedback resulted in Jane's assumption that these skills would also serve her well as a principal in this new situation. Here, again, Jane failed to consider one of the key principles affecting her effectiveness. She had gotten feedback and thought she knew how to approach the faculty. Had she considered what she already knew about herself in light of this new situation and new group of constituents, she might have questioned whether the old techniques would work as well as they had in her former position. She would have analyzed the match between the leadership needs of the school and her own skills. She might have realized that extra care should have been taken to ensure that her intent was accurately communicated in a letter that would determine the first impression her new faculty would have of her.

Emotion as a Factor

Emotion played a significant role in this situation. Jane failed to consider the emotional impact of change. She was energized by what she perceived as a positive change for her and assumed that her constituents would feel the same. Change generally sparks a negative reaction. People involved in change feel a sense of loss and need assurance that all they have done before was not a failure. This emotional impact can be clearly seen in all three key elements we presented in chapter 2. It certainly influenced Tom as he read Jane's letter. He was already dealing with the emotions that typically accompany change: a sense of rejection and uncertainty about what he could or should do, as well as other emotional issues. The emotion embedded in the situation is evident in the new school, the new leader, the need to form new relationships, the issues surrounding accountability, and other like feelings that are tied to the situation at this school. Finally, emotion is a crucial part of Jane's actions and reactions. She is excited about being a principal. She wants to make a good first impression and has reached out to the faculty thinking she will be welcomed as an energetic, excited, instructional leader. When she sees that Tom and other faculty have not reacted as she expects, her emotions will certainly come into play. If she is not careful, the situation will get worse because of her emotional reaction to this rejection. Let's see what happens.

The Cycle Continues

When the special teachers' meeting takes place, Jane is in a very bad mood. She has received several calls from teachers who reacted to her letter as Tom did. Some of the teachers who called were very angry about the meeting and said they planned to call their association representative about being paid. Jane also received a call from the superintendent about her letter and the spelling error. He had made it clear that the district did not require teachers to report prior to the first workday and had no funds to pay supplements. Jane also discovered that student schedules had not been done, school supplies had not been ordered, and last-minute details were taking all of her time. She had worked late into the night and on weekends for the past two weeks. She was stressed and exhausted. Her feelings were dominating her. As the few teachers who decided to attend the meeting arrived, Jane greeted them. She tried to be positive and upbeat, but her nonverbal behavior betrayed her stress and exhaustion. She was just too exhausted to be convincing. Mindful that she still had hours of work yet to do, she rushed through some comments she had hurriedly prepared. She had not had time to prepare for this meeting and, on several occasions, she paused uncomfortably as she searched her notes. She totally forgot about the state test and made no mention of it. As she rushed through her comments, she could see that the teachers in attendance were not impressed with their new principal.

Jane's perception of the teachers' reactions was on target. They wondered why they had bothered to come to the meeting. Some had heard the criticism directed at Jane and had decided to come to support her. Others had come to check Jane out. Both groups left the school with doubts about their new principal's ability to lead.

Jane's Reflection

Sitting in her office after the meeting, Jane began to reflect on her situation. She realized that she had made some mistakes. She wished that she could start over, but she knew that she could not. Jane knew that she would have to overcome the initial impression she had made on her new constituents. In addition to her failure to consider the new situation she was facing, her new constituents, the qualities she brought with her, and the role emotional intelligence would play in her success, Jane also reflected on how her skill or lack of skill affected her situation. As she thought, it became increasingly clear to her that leadership skills were a crucial part of being an effective principal.

SKILLS AND THEIR IMPACT ON LEADERSHIP EFFECTIVENESS

In chapter 2, we addressed trait theory. You will recall that we listed trait theory as one of the many failed leadership theories, but we also suggested that many of the things we have learned about leadership are useful. We feel that what we know about the relationship between skills and leader effectiveness provides you with a useful tool. Effective leaders possess many skills that help them be more effective. The skills that have been identified through trait theory when combined with emotional intelligence provide opportunities to increase understanding of self.

Trait theory attempts to discover the traits (skills, knowledge, dispositions, etc.) that ensure any leader's effectiveness. The problem with trait theory is that situations, constituents, self, and emotional intelligence make the variables leaders face so complex that no set of descriptors can hope to be comprehensive enough to cover them all. Leaders need to build their own set of essential skills for each situation and group of constituents. Skills help us understand ourselves better. Skills define the things that leaders do to be effective in the situations in which they find themselves. Skills may be viewed as a cookbook for effective leadership because they help us ensure that all the ingredients are included.

Take Jane's situation, for example. She would have been well served had she used the skill of problem analysis prior to writing her letter. Problem analysis is a generic skill that can be found on most effective leadership trait lists. Typically, problem analysis is described as the ability to know that additional information is needed and to know where to find appropriate information for the situation at hand. Had she used this skill effectively, Jane would have discovered that her new constituents were sensitive about the state test, had been involved in the design of the new building, and were apprehensive about moving to a new school with a new leader. Had she then used this information to write a more appropriate letter (this is another skill typically called judgment or decision making), the outcome might have been very different. We say *might have* because using these two skills does not guarantee success. Jane would still have to communicate in a manner that would be perceived as sensitive by her new constituents to obtain the results she wanted.

Sensitivity is another skill that appears on many lists of traits for effective leaders. It is frequently a misunderstood trait. Many leaders who are told they should be sensitive assume that means they should always put their constituents' wishes first. Some assume being sensitive means always saying yes to requests. Others think it means having genuine feelings of concern for others. The skill of sensitivity actually has as much to do with how others perceive you as it has to do with how you actually feel. We are not suggesting that you should develop a façade of sensitivity to gain the approval or support of your constituents. We are suggesting that leaders like Jane can be perceived to be less sensitive than they actually are. Jane's goal was to use the letter and meeting to show her constituents how much she cared about them, but she made several mistakes that caused her to be perceived differently. Some knowledge of skills that might influence a leader's effectiveness would have been a useful tool. Jane could have referred to it as she moved into her new position to ensure that she was being as effective as she had been in her old position. For example, Jane's energy and openness will continue to be an asset in the new school, but her failure to analyze her new situation created a situation in which her skills worked against her. Had she sought out some of the information we described earlier, she could have scheduled meetings with teachers, like Tom, individually. At those meetings, she could have used her energy to convey to these teachers her desire to work with them and to be the principal they wanted her to be.

What Skills Affect a School Leader's Effectiveness?

You might be wondering where you could find a list of skills to modify for your situation. Fortunately, several lists have been compiled specifically for school leaders. The National Association of Secondary School Principals (NASSP) began assessing the skills of potential leaders in 1975. Working with the American Psychological Association, the NASSP identified twelve skills (see table 4.1) that were factors in a principal's success. The skills and simulations participants confronted were focused primarily on the management tasks principals encountered prior to recent reforms in which instructional leadership came into vogue. During the past quarter century, new assessment programs have been developed by NASSP that include instructional leadership. The National Association of Elementary School Principals (NAESP) also has developed an assessment process for school leaders. These assessment programs are useful tools that can greatly increase understanding of strengths and weaknesses. We feel that participation in one of these programs enables a school leader to better apply the models in this book.

As the importance of instructional leadership increased, additional skill lists were developed for school leaders. These lists generally included some of the skills from the NASSP and NAESP skill lists with some additions aimed at the principal's role as an instructional leader. One list was created under the direction of the National Policy Board for Educational Administration (NPBEA). The NPBEA 21 Domains expanded the skills and traits to include areas that were beginning to take on more importance. They were primarily designed for use in graduate principal preparation programs.

The most recent addition to trait theory for school leaders has come from the Interstate School Leaders Licensure Consortium (ISLLC). This is the most diverse group to date to develop a list of expectations for school leaders. In addition to the NPBEA, ISLLC drew participation from over thirty states. The two-year process that produced the ISLLC Standards for School Leaders involved representatives from all the major education administration associations and many state departments of public education. These standards were developed in the hope that they would drive the political agenda of school reform that was sweeping the nation. The standards were created in order to put the focus squarely on the school leader's responsibility to be an instructional leader. The six standards were broad-sweeping statements. The real meat in these new standards is found in the indicators for knowledge, disposition, and performance included with each standard. In particular, the indicators of performance contain clear expectations for current and future school leaders. The complete listing of standards and indicators is contained in Appendix C.

Table 4.1. The Original NASSP Assessment Center Skills

Problem Analysis	Ability to seek out relevant data and analyze complex information to determine the important elements of a problem situation, searching for information with a purpose.
Judgment	Ability to reach logical conclusions and make high-quality decisions based on available information; skill in identifying problems based on available information; skill in identifying educational needs based on available information; skill in identifying educational needs and setting priorities; ability to critically evaluate written communications.
Organizational Ability	Ability to plan, schedule, and control the work of others; skill in using resources in an optimal fashion; ability to deal with a volume of paperwork.
Decisiveness	Ability to recognize when a decision is required (disregarding the quality of the decision) and to act quickly.
Leadership	Ability to get others involved in solving problems; ability to recognize when a group requires direction; to interact with a group effectively and to guide them to the accomplishment of a task.
Sensitivity	Ability to perceive the needs, concerns, and personal problems of others; skill in resolving conflicts; tact in dealing with persons from different backgrounds; ability to deal effectively with people concerning emotional issues; knowing what information to communicate and to whom.
Stress Tolerance	Ability to perform under pressure and during opposition; ability to think on one's feet.
Oral Communication	Ability to make a clear oral presentation of facts and ideas.
Written Communication	Ability to express ideas in writing; to write appropriately for different audiences—students, teachers, parents, et al.
Range of Interest	Competence to discuss a variety of subjects—educational, political, current events, economic, etc.; desire to actively participate in events.
Personal Motivation	Need to achieve in all activities attempted; evidence that work is important to personal satisfaction; ability to be self-policing.
Educational Values	Possession of a well-reasoned educational philosophy; receptive to new ideas and change.

There is a problem, however, with using these standards for development. They are written in outcome language rather than skill indicator terminology. For example, the first performance indicator under standard 1 states, "The administrator facilitates, processes, and engages in activities ensuring that the vision and mission of the school are effectively communicated to staff, parents, students, and community members." This indicator gives clear guidance regarding the importance of communicating the school vision to a wide audience, but it gives no clues about how to accomplish this feat. In other words, what should a leader do to make sure the vision of the school is effectively communicated to all? These standards are more like evaluation criteria than a skills list. That is, in fact, exactly how they are being used—to serve as the basis for a licensure exam and administrator evaluation instruments.

The ISLLC Standards provide guidance regarding the central focus of school leadership instruction. They provide food for thought regarding the things that school leaders should value and the goals to which they should strive. When combined with an analysis of the skills needed to accomplish these indicators and consideration of situations, constituents, self, and emotional intelligence, they can be helpful tools for a school leader.

SUMMARY

In this chapter, we looked at the skills that affect a school leader's effectiveness. We looked at a new leader who unknowingly made crucial mistakes in a new position. She used skills that had served her well in the past, but because she did not consider the situation, her new constituents, and emotional factors, these skills were not effective. Reflection on what happened led this new leader to the realization that skills are important. The lists of skills for school leaders that have been developed can be useful tools for those who want to use them for self-analysis. Skill lists can never define all the attributes school leaders need in all situations, but they can help us define the key skills needed in individual situations and help us assess our strengths and weaknesses. Finally, several skill lists and the ISLLC Standards for school leaders were reviewed.

FIVE FAST FUNDAMENTALS FROM THIS CHAPTER

1. Knowledge of specific skills and skill sets is essential in school leadership.
2. Lists of skills developed by school leadership organizations can be useful in pinpointing specific, necessary skills.
3. The skills of problem analysis are particularly useful when encountering unfamiliar situations.
4. Interpersonal skill sets track closely with skills based in the emotions.
5. Lists of skills are rarely comprehensive but they can define key skills for specific situations.

CHAPTER 5

Instructional Leadership: The New Challenge

In a bygone era, school leaders who kept their schools clean and orderly (which included such tasks as aligning all the blinds along the front of the school at the same level) were considered successful. That era ended when the accountability movement began and became the driving force in education. The new era began when the report *A Nation at Risk* (1983) documented the public's growing dissatisfaction with public education and sounded the call for a new way of viewing the success of schools and their leaders. Administrators who had long understood the importance of teaching and learning welcomed the calls for instructional leadership embedded in the accountability movement. Those who had survived solely on their management skills and were unwilling to change found their work increasingly difficult and stressful. As schools have moved further into this new era and into a new millennium, the calls for effective instructional leadership in the nation's schools have grown even louder. This chapter focuses on the school leader's role as an instructional leader. We address the relationships between emotional intelligence, situations, constituents, and leadership qualities associated with instructional leadership.

NEW RULES FOR LEADERS

The ISLLC Standards we discussed earlier are clear evidence of the importance of instructional leadership. These standards stress instructional leadership that is student-centered with teaching and learning at its core. They also signal that school leaders must be collaborative as they work with and through school staff, parents, and the entire school community to improve their schools. This trend toward more collaborative school leadership has mirrored a similar trend in thinking about leadership in general. Leaders of organizations, including schools, are now being judged by how they serve their customers, increase quality without increasing cost, bring about change to meet new challenges, and organize employees to function in the most effective manner possible. This shift rewards leaders who are effective in fast-changing organizations staffed by a new kind of worker who can think and who expects to participate in decision making in an atmosphere where outcomes are the measure of a leader's effectiveness.

Student achievement is the outcome by which a school leader's success is most often measured. Yet a school leader affects the instructional program indirectly by working through others—the teachers and other staff who deliver most of the instruction in schools. Leaders greatly improve their chances for success if they involve others in decision making about how to improve student performance. As decisions are made regarding how instruction can be improved, it is essential to engage those who will do the work in making the decisions about how the work should be done. This situation has changed traditional relationships, changed the way leaders are evaluated, and changed the things leaders need to know and are able to do. We address this shift to put into focus the situations, constituents, and traditional roles school leaders have played. Few have framed these new realities better than Carolyn Kelley. Writing in the *Educational Administration Quarterly*, she describes current expectations of school leaders:

> Although accountability is not new to education, the current educational accountability movement represents a significant shift in policy focus from accountability for resource use to accountability for outcomes produced. This shift in focus creates numerous technical and political challenges that need to be overcome, including negotiating agreement about what outcomes are most valued, developing technologies adequate to assess and system capacity adequate to produce these valued outcomes, and designing effective incentives structured to motivate complex behavioral changes. Research evidence to date suggests that the valued outcomes are contested, technologies are often inadequate, the system lacks capacity, and the design of incentive structures is tricky. In short,

> improving student achievement using accountability within the current context might be likened to trying to build a Stradivarius violin with a sledgehammer, a chisel, and a number of apprentice technicians who disagree on how to proceed. The desired outcome—significant improvement in student achievement—may be unattainable using available tools, resources, and system capacity. (Kelley 1999, 642–43)

Kelley certainly paints a dismal picture. Yet this challenging era in school leadership also offers many opportunities for leaders who understand themselves, their constituents, and the situations they face. Never before have school leaders had such an opportunity to make significant changes in their schools. In the past, innovative leaders could be outlasted by constituents unwilling to change. Today, change is the rule rather than the exception. Success is determined by how effectively leaders manage situations, constituents, and self. These key elements, identified in previous chapters, are crucial pieces of the puzzle whose solution leads to improved schools.

INSTRUCTIONAL LEADERSHIP

How Much Should You Know?

Before we address emotional intelligence, we need to address another intelligence. How much does a school leader need to know about teaching and learning in order to be an effective school leader? This question is not easily answered. The ISLLC Standards include knowledge indicators, but they might not be adequate for all situations. Few suggest that school leaders need to know the content of each subject as well as the teachers know it, but most agree, as do we, that school leaders should thoroughly understand teaching. In addition, instructional leaders must seek out new instructional techniques that will improve the quality of teaching in their schools. Brain research holds the promise of helping us better understand the teaching and learning process. Instructional leaders must stay abreast of discoveries that can help them improve the teaching and learning in their schools.

A number of lists are available to school leaders who want to increase their understanding of effective teaching. These lists serve to define effective teaching in a wide variety of ways. Most states have defined teacher effectiveness through their teacher evaluation instruments or through standards for teachers. State teaching expectations are a resource for instructional leaders who want to better understand effective teaching.

Beginning teachers are one group of teachers dependent on the support of an instructional leader. These teachers face increased pressure in this era of accountability. Most beginning teachers struggle with classroom management and other issues during their first years in the classroom. Without the support of an instructional leader, their chances for success are limited. Statistics reveal that beginning teachers leave the profession at a high rate. Successful instructional leaders understand the need and importance of supporting their beginning teachers in general, but in an era of teacher shortage, this need and importance is amplified. Fortunately, the Interstate New Teacher Assessment and Support Consortium (INTASC) has developed a set of standards specifically for beginning teachers. The INTASC Standards are one of the tools instructional leaders may use to better understand and support teachers. The complete INTASC Standards are listed in Appendix C.

At the other end of the spectrum are the National Board Standards for Teacher Certification. This set of standards is used to certify master teachers nationally and represents the highest level of teaching performance. The standards inform instructional leaders about effective teaching practice at the highest levels. Together, the National Board Standards and the INTASC Standards frame the behaviors and techniques of effective teaching at the beginning and master levels. Instructional leaders must understand effective teaching practice. Even though our focus will be on how to work with teachers and others to improve instruction, we want to stress the need to gain knowledge of best practice and the need to stay informed regarding innovations in teaching and learning techniques and methodologies.

These national teacher standards provide instructional leaders with information about effective teaching. The standards address the delivery of subject content as well as teachers' needs to master subject content. We feel that the delivery of subject content is the crucial factor. Teachers must know their content, but knowing content does not guarantee effective instruction. Many teachers who know their subjects are still not effective in the classroom. Inadequate student performance rarely results from a teacher's lack of content knowledge. The root problem with low student performance is more typically inadequate instructional delivery. We therefore suggest that the major task for the instructional leader is improving instructional delivery. The instructional leader's ability to help teachers improve their instructional delivery is often the measure of a leader's success.

Instructional Leaders and Their Constituents

We suggest that helping teachers improve their effectiveness is the most important and challenging task instructional leaders face. The process through which leaders help teachers improve their performance involves all the key elements we have identified. The teacher, as the constituent, certainly brings emotion to the situation. Accurate assessment of the teacher's feelings and appropriate responses to those feelings are critical factors in an instructional leader's success. The situation in which teachers and instructional leaders find themselves also influences their emotions. Finally, the instructional leader's approach, determined by skills, disposition, and self-perception, play a crucial role. These interrelated factors are best demonstrated by reviewing an actual situation and examining each element in action.

A Promising New Teacher

Juan has just finished his first observation in Ms. Washington's class. He worked hard to win the recruiting war for Ms. Washington, who won the Outstanding Teacher Intern Award at her university while interning in his school. Even though she had done her internship at his school and worked with one of his best teachers, Juan had to compete with some of the state's highest paying school districts to sign her to a contract. In the final analysis, Ms. Washington's desire to work with less privileged students and the wonderful experience she had as an intern were the key factors in her decision to stay with Juan. As he walked back to his office, Juan wondered what happened to the wonderful intern who had worked in his school last year. The class he just visited was nothing like the classes he visited when Ms. Washington was interning. The students were off task and Ms. Washington seemed unable to engage the students in her lesson. All the hands-on activities Ms. Washington had used effectively last year were gone and she was now lecturing. As Juan considered what to do next, he remembered the situation Ms. Washington entered last year.

As an intern, Ms. Washington had worked with one of the best teachers in the school. Ms. Clark, a veteran of twenty years and Ms. Washington's mentor, had mastered the art of teaching and could engage students in meaningful learning experiences, regardless of their background or skill level. Juan recalled that last year was the year he had decided to reward Ms. Clark with some of his better students and to provide an intern to lighten her load. Prior to Ms. Washington's arrival, Ms. Clark had worked her usual magic with the class and when Ms. Washington arrived, the students already understood the teacher's behavioral expectations and were actively engaged in learning. Ms. Washington had not observed Ms. Clark as she had begun the year and made her expectations clear to the students. Nor had Ms. Washington seen how Ms. Clark had worked with the students to prepare them prior to her arrival. Working from her perceptions as an intern, Ms. Washington had begun the year just as she had begun as an intern. She did the same things that had worked so well last year and when they failed, she did not know what to do. She had never been in this situation before and must have felt added pressure because she had been recognized as the Outstanding Teacher Intern. Juan reflected on how lonely and isolated Ms. Washington must be feeling.

The situation was further exacerbated by the state's new beginning teacher induction program that was designed to support new teachers, but also included high expectations. Soon, Ms. Washington would have to begin to collect artifacts to document her teaching successes, but she had few artifacts that demonstrated teaching success. In addition, she taught a grade in which students would be taking a state test that would determine if they would be promoted to the next grade. The pressures Ms. Washington felt must have seemed to increase daily. The more overwhelmed she felt, the more she withdrew from her colleagues, fearing they would discover how lost she was.

Juan understood the emotional elements in the situation Ms. Washington faced because he carefully analyzed what had happened rather than rushing to judgment. The ability to accurately analyze problems was a strength Juan often exhibited. Juan had gotten feedback on this strength through an assessment activity and through feedback from colleagues and peers. He also knew that his ability to work with subordinates was limited because he had difficulty projecting his concerns. As Juan thought about how best to help Ms. Washington, his understanding of his own limitations weighed heavily on his mind. To help Ms. Washington, Juan would have to effectively use his strengths to compensate for his weaknesses.

EFFECTIVE INSTRUCTIONAL LEADERSHIP

Instructional leadership, at its most basic level, is about improving the quality of instruction in a school. To improve instructional quality, school leaders must work with teachers, students, parents, and other members of the school community. This process includes hundreds of interactions in which school leaders face situations similar to the one Juan faced. Their success is greatly influenced by the manner in which they assess the emotions of the people with whom they interact, the emotions embedded in the situations, and the personal factors they bring to the situation.

Assessing Emotional Factors in Others

Juan could have approached Ms. Washington and her problem from a very different perspective. Having seen how effective she had been, Juan could have assumed that her problems were the result of a lack of motivation, emotional problems, or some other factor unrelated to the actual situation. If he had not accurately assessed the problem and the emotional factors affecting Ms. Washington, it is likely that she would be added to the list of beginning teachers who leave the profession because they feel that they are not supported by the administration. So what did Juan do to accurately assess the problem and the emotional factors with which Ms. Washington was dealing?

Juan has an advantage because he is a skilled problem analyzer. This built-in advantage enabled him to identify the data he needed prior to making a decision about Ms. Washington and her problems. Fortunately, all school leaders can develop this skill and it begins with not making assumptions that are not supported by facts or sound reasoning. As Juan reflected on what he had observed in the class, he thought about possible reasons. He did not immediately assume that Ms. Washington was not putting forth her best effort or that she had been overrated the previous year. Instead, he tried to figure out why this year's class was so different from last year's class. Juan knew that people generally do their best and that they do what they know how to do. This willing suspension of blame is an important element in accurately assessing an instructional problem. Next, Juan carefully reviewed the events that had occurred, both last year and this year. This analysis helped him see that Ms. Washington faced a very different environment this year and that she had not had the opportunity to learn many things that could have helped her in her current situation. He also accurately assessed her current emotional state. It would have been easy for him to assume that she resisted contact with her peers because she thought she was superior. Withdrawal or unwillingness to accept offers of help are common characteristics of individuals who feel embarrassed by their inadequacies or fear that they will be seen as incompetent. Juan's success in trying to help Ms. Washington will be influenced greatly by his skill in dealing with her emotions. His next step will be to test these assumptions about Ms. Washington's feelings and learn more about her emotional state.

Checklist for Assessing Emotional Factors in Others

The following checklist is designed to assist instructional leaders as they assess the emotional factors in others. This list is not intended to be inclusive of all the factors that might come into play in a situation. We therefore encourage you to develop your own list of key attributes for your situation. We hope this list will be helpful as you develop your list.

- How might my emotions affect my assessment?
- How can I ensure that my emotions will not skew my assessment?
- Who can/should assist with this analysis?
- What are the possible causes for behaviors?
- What data is needed to identify the actual cause of this problem?
- How can the needed data be gathered?

- What types of data need to be gathered?
- Does the data include information about the emotional states of individuals who will be affected by the action taken?
- How much data is needed before a decision can be made?
- How can the accuracy of the decision be judged?

Assessing Emotional Factors in the Situation

Juan's efforts to help this teacher will be influenced by factors in the situation surrounding them both. It is important to note that constituent, situational, and leader factors often overlap and become interrelated in ways that make separation difficult or impossible. If you are having difficulty categorizing factors, remember that it makes little difference how you categorize. What is important is that you consider as many of the factors that will lead to success and improved instruction as possible.

The unique situational factors Juan and Ms. Washington face include the state's accountability program and the state's program to license beginning teachers. They could also include the students currently in her class, the teaching materials available, her relationship with other teachers, and other factors. The analysis of situational factors should include all the things that affect instruction and the emotions of those who are involved. Initially, the manner in which situations affect Ms. Washington's emotions are the focal point of the analysis. As the analysis of situational factors surrounding Ms. Washington is concluded and a plan to address the problem is developed, it will be important to continue to analyze situational factors that will affect others involved in the plan. For example, if the decision is made to ask Ms. Clark to mentor Ms. Washington, it would be important to consider the emotional impact this would have on her and the situation. This is as important as considering the factors that will affect Ms. Washington. The state testing and licensure programs are situational factors Juan is powerless to change. He can, however, take action to help Ms. Washington deal with these aspects of the situation. This analysis will also reveal things that are within his power to change.

The factors in the situations instructional leaders face generally manifest themselves in the emotional reactions of constituents or leaders themselves. To exclude the consideration of situations and only consider the emotions of constituents, or leaders, would be a mistake. Situation-embedded emotions are difficult to understand if the situation itself is not a part of the analysis.

Checklist for Assessing Situational Factors

The following checklist is designed to assist instructional leaders as they assess the situational factors. This list is not intended to be inclusive of all factors that might come into play in a situation. We again encourage you to develop your own list of key attributes for situations you encounter. We hope this list will be helpful as you develop your list.

- What is new or different about the situation?
- What data is needed to understand this situation?
- Who can/should assist in the gathering of data?
- What are the possible causes for this situation?
- How can bias be eliminated from the information about this situation?
- How can the emotional impact of the situation be assessed?
- What will indicate that enough data has been gathered to fully understand the emotional aspects of the situational changes?
- What can be changed in the situation?
- What can be done if the situation cannot be changed?

Assessing Emotional Factors in Yourself

As a part of his assessment of factors influencing Ms. Washington and the situation she faced, Juan included himself. You will recall that his reflections about the teacher and her situation also included reflections about his strengths as a problem analyzer and his weakness in communicating his concerns to others. Had he stopped with an analysis of Ms. Washington and the situation, Juan might have attempted to interact with the teacher in an effort to help her regain her lost effectiveness. Had he done so, his success would have been limited by his failure to consider how he would have influenced the situation personally. His reflections about his strengths and weaknesses are only the beginning of the needed analysis. Further analysis is needed regarding Juan's feelings about the situation, Ms. Washington, the impact of other situations affecting Juan and the school, and many other factors.

Checklist for Assessing Self Factors

The following checklist is designed to assist instructional leaders as they assess themselves. This list is not intended to be inclusive of all the factors that might come into play in a given situation. We again encourage you to develop your own list of key attributes for situations you encounter. We hope this list will be helpful as you develop your list.

- What strengths and weaknesses do I bring to this situation?
- How can my strengths be employed to improve instruction?
- What strategies should be implemented to allow me to compensate for my weaknesses?
- What is my emotional reaction to the situation?
- What role will my emotional reaction play in improving instruction?
- How can I monitor my emotional reactions?

SUMMARY

The importance of instructional leadership has increased significantly as a result of the accountability movement sweeping the nation. New standards for school leaders reflect the increased importance of teaching and learning. Knowledge of effective teaching practice as it is defined in national and state standards is essential for instructional leaders. Knowledge about effective practice, however, is only part of what school leaders must have to be effective. In this new era of school accountability, school leaders must be able to analyze their situations, constituents, and selves. Being an effective instructional leader includes being able to diagnose the emotions embedded in situations, others, and self, and taking actions that are tailored to meet the unique needs provided by all three factors.

FIVE FAST FUNDAMENTALS FROM THIS CHAPTER

1. Exercising instructional leadership is the most crucial situation faced by school leaders.
2. Instructional leaders must understand and be able to articulate the learning process.
3. Emotion is an important element in the teaching and learning process.
4. The INTASC Standards provide a helpful guide to effective teaching.
5. Checklists for assessing emotional factors in constituents, situations, and self are also helpful in managing specific situations.

CHAPTER 6

Ethical Leadership: More Important Than Ever

The basic premise of this chapter is that good leadership and ethical leadership are synonymous. There is no contradiction between leading effectively and practicing moral leadership. The exercise of moral behavior and the articulation of ethical educational values is not only the right thing to do, it is an essential part of educational leadership.

Twenty-five years ago, when both authors were studying educational administration, most leadership theorists emphasized a slightly different focus in educational administration. At that time, ethics in leadership were usually relegated to a brief passage near the end of the school management textbooks. If you had been able to talk off the record to many school superintendents and principals, they would probably have admitted that a Machiavellian viewpoint prevailed when considering the moral aspects of leadership. Machiavelli, of course, proclaimed that the end justified the means. You did what you had to do to achieve your objective even if what you had to do was unscrupulous (e.g., lying or misleading). We are not saying that bad or unethical people were administering schools twenty-five years ago. There was a general belief then, however, that when it came to certain aspects of school administration, you could not survive if you were a "goody two-shoes," someone who was not aware of the hard realities of management life. Recently, leadership theorists such as Sergiovanni (1992) and Maxcy (1991) have eloquently stated the need for the consideration of ethical concerns in the practice of school leadership. They have pointed out the inherent moral nature of school leadership. The very act of leading schools and school systems has strong moral dimensions that leaders must consider.

Why the current emphasis on moral leadership? Four issues drive the interest in moral leadership.

1. Researchers are finding strong correlations between effective leadership and ethical leadership.
2. Constituents are better informed than in the past, so unethical leadership conduct is more obvious than in the past.
3. Schools have become a forum for many of the moral controversies and ethical debates present in the larger society.
4. Articulation of the ethical principles of the school and school system is becoming a basic function of leadership and this function can only be performed by the leader of the school or school system.

LEADERSHIP AND HONESTY

Research

Kouzes and Posner (1993) provided empirical support for the importance of ethical leadership behavior. They asked constituents in business, education, and industry to identify the most important characteristic these constituents valued in their leaders. Honesty was the most frequently cited characteristic. Kouzes and Posner used these findings to make the case that credibility is a fundamental prerequisite for effective leadership. They defined credibility as a combination of honesty and competence. The credible leader is someone who knows what he is doing and tells the truth about it. Leaders who possess credibility gained the trust of their constituents. And here, once again, we come to the subject of emotions in leadership.

Trust: A Powerful Leadership Emotion

Trust is a very strong emotion but is very difficult to assess and measure, and thus is often overlooked in discussions of leadership. Yet trust is real and has a powerful effect on any organization. As stated in chapter 1, emotions move people to action. Trust can move people within a group to behavior that is productive and beneficial for the group. Think about any group of which you were a part. If you had a good experience working with that group, be it a football team, sewing circle, or bridge club, wasn't trust in the group a large part of your good experience? Now think about any group with whom you had a bad experience. Wasn't there a lack of trust within that group? You could not rely on the word of the leader or other members of the group, and working with this particular group of people was often an unpleasant experience.

Although unethical or unscrupulous leadership might work for a short time or in a specific situation, good leadership is characterized by moral behavior over the long haul. Reflect upon leaders you have known personally, leaders for whom you were willing to sacrifice your time, effort, sweat, and to whom you gladly gave the most precious thing, except love, that any human can give another: your work. These leaders were all people you could trust. Their word, once given, you believed. In contrast, think of leaders you have known whose word could not be trusted, who said they would do one thing but did another. These leaders you could not trust when things went wrong. Over the long term, these leaders were not effective.

Effects of the Information Explosion

Today we are flooded with information from many different sources. Easy access to the Internet, twenty-four-hour news networks, and specialty publications in fields as diverse as numismatics and dog breeding make for a highly informed citizenry. Often, unethical leadership is characterized by the manipulation of information. Manipulating information in the "Age of Information" is becoming increasingly difficult. When constituents are well informed and have access to diverse sources of knowledge, controlling access to information is a difficult alternative. Consequently, at national, state, and local levels, we are aware of unacceptable conduct on the part of leaders. We talked earlier of the value of networking. Teachers and other education constituents are also aware of networking and freely trade information about working conditions, budgets, career opportunities, and school leaders. This information exchange further limits the unscrupulous leader's ability to maneuver in an unethical manner. Educator networks alert other educators to examples of bad leadership behavior. The net result of the information explosion is to raise awareness of unethical leadership behavior and thus make ethical leadership a more valued commodity.

ETHICS IN AN EDUCATIONAL SETTING

Schools as Arenas for Moral Conflict

The school has become a forum for many of the moral controversies and ethical debates present in the larger society. Arguments about birth control versus the practice of abstinence, debates about prayer in schools, and controversies about distributing scarce educational resources to haves or have-nots must be faced by principals, superintendents, directors, and supervisors on a daily basis. School administrators are slowly discovering that simply assuming a position of neutrality when these controversies arise does not serve their interests or the interests of their school or school system. Taking a position of neutrality on issues of moral significance does not distinguish them as school leaders.

Leaders who either have no position or are reluctant to state their position on issues that have a major impact on students in the schools are seen as moral ciphers, lacking beliefs and convictions. In attempting not to offend either side of a moral debate, leaders, unwilling to state their moral convictions, anger both sides and lose the respect of the larger school community. Dante said that the hottest places in hell were reserved for those who do not take a position during a time of moral crisis. There is simply no place to hide from the moral storms that are a constant presence in schools and school systems.

The prevailing belief that modern-day leaders in all fields, including politics, business, and education, are not forthright and candid about their beliefs puts a premium on leaders who are unafraid to stand by their core principles. Recall the 2000 election and the candidacy of John McCain. Although his political organization was outspent and out-organized by George W. Bush's campaign, voters were attracted to McCain's candidacy. Many voters did not agree with McCain's positions but were drawn by his courage in stating his beliefs and the forceful and persuasive way in which he articulated his core principles.

We live in an age of specialization. School systems employ legal specialists to handle legal issues. Financial specialists are hired to make prudent decisions about school finance. No one is employed by the school system to analyze and articulate the school's or school system's educational principles. This job is left to the school leader.

Analyzing and Articulating Educational Principles

Only the principal can state with authority what his or her school stands for. Only the superintendent can articulate the school district's position on the issue of educating every student in the district. We do not suggest that stating a moral position and standing behind that position is an easy task. Before educational principles can be articulated, an ethical analysis must be conducted. All school leaders are capable of performing ethical analysis with prior preparation and the knowledge that the emotions play a key role in the moral aspects of any situation. The remainder of this chapter covers a simple formula for ethical analysis. Once an ethical analysis is accomplished, the articulation of the moral principles and values that form the basis for a moral position can be done with precision and confidence.

THE POTTER'S BOX

The Potter's box, as described by Christians, Rotzoll, and Fackler (1983), offers a straightforward, uncomplicated method of moral analysis. School leaders are often too busy for time-consuming philosophical musings, but it is important that school administrators consider the moral aspects of leadership problems and it is important that they articulate moral and ethical principles when explaining decisions and actions. Many school leaders are uncomfortable when discussing moral issues. The Potter's box affords the school leader the opportunity to employ an ethical vocabulary and utilize concepts such as fairness, justice, and truth to articulate educational principles and explain moral perspectives.

Dr. Ralph Potter, a Harvard Divinity School professor, developed the model upon which the Potter's box is based. The Potter's box is a heuristic analytical process that can be used to study four dimensions of a moral problem. The four aspects of a moral dilemma scrutinized in the Potter's box are shown in figure 6.1.

FACTS	MORAL PRINCIPLES
VALUES	LOYALTIES

Figure 6.1. Potter's Box

The Potter's box assumes that, if a moral dilemma exists, there is some conflict between competing moral principles, values, or loyalties. Therefore, it is necessary to describe the facts in the situation and then analyze the moral principles, loyalties, and values to determine the source of conflicts.

In order to use the Potter's box, we must first define the ethical terminology used in the box:

- Facts: A statement of the ethical problem we are considering. The facts are a general description of the ethical dilemma with which we are confronted.
- Values and Moral Principles: Strike, Haller, and Soltis (1998) contend that the difference between values and moral principles is that one can justly compel others to adhere to moral principles but values are a matter of personal choice. For example, a moral principle is that one should not lie. Not only should I not lie to you, I can also demand that you do not lie to me. If either of us does choose to lie, we will not be able to communicate because we will not know what to believe. A value, on the other hand, is a matter of personal choice. I like oranges, whereas you may like apples. I will not compel you to eat oranges just because I like them. Examples of moral principles are:

    1. The Judeo-Christian ethos asserts that all people, no matter what their station in life, have dignity and worth because they are created in the image of God.

2. Kant's categorical imperative asserts that what is right for one should be right for all.
3. Mill's principle of utilitarianism asserts that one should seek the greatest good for the greatest number.

- Loyalties: Loyalties determine where our allegiances lie. Our loyalties dictate which side we favor in a moral dispute.

We will now describe a common dilemma confronted frequently by school administrators and use the Potter's box to analyze that problem from an ethical perspective.

Example Utilizing the Potter's Box

The Situation

An experienced high school science teacher was once a talented educator. The teacher has experienced many personal problems in the last few years involving illness and the loss of loved ones and is no longer an effective teacher. The teacher's ineffectiveness has been demonstrated through test scores of the teacher's students and by the observations of supervisors. Supervisory interventions have not helped the teacher regain teaching effectiveness. Now, a once-capable and admired educator is incompetent and three years from retirement. The teacher works with over 140 students every semester.

Ethical Analysis Using the Potter's Box

- Facts:
  (A) A talented teacher is no longer effective because of personal problems
  (B) Intervention has not worked
- Conflicting Values:
  (A) Value placed on the welfare of a colleague
  (B) Value placed on the instructional program
- Conflicting Moral Principles:
  (A) Judeo-Christian Ethos. Teacher should be treated with dignity and respect.

(B) Mill's Utilitarianism. What is the greatest good for the greatest number? One hundred forty students' education is being harmed.

- Loyalties:
  (A) To Students
  (B) To the Teacher

In this brief, shorthand analysis, the basic ethical conflicts are clearly delineated. A conflict in values exists between the value of a professional colleague and the value placed on an instructional program that is harmed by the teacher's continued ineffectiveness. A conflict occurs when the moral principle of the dignity and worth of individuals (because of the teacher's possible dismissal) is balanced against the educational damage to more than one hundred students if the teacher is not removed from the classroom. And finally, a conflict in loyalties exists between loyalty to the teacher and loyalty to the students. The Potter's box offers a graphic illustration of why this situation, one that occurs in hundreds of school systems every year, is so difficult to deal with, and why it is often mishandled. It is a truly compelling moral dilemma because both moral principles are valid and owed some consideration. Both the teacher and the educational program should be valued and both parties in the situation are owed loyalty. The Potter's box does not purport to solve the problem but it does clearly illustrate the parameters of the problem and provides the terminology and vocabulary that must be used when the problem is discussed and the eventual decision explained.

We do not contend that the Potter's box is a substitute for deep philosophical inquiry. Nor do we assert that there is no need for administrators to be familiar with classical philosophy and moral instruction. In the hectic press of events that every educational leader encounters, time is a major concern. The Potter's box is a sound and uncomplicated method of ethical analysis. The Potter's box allows ethical inquiry to be conducted in a brief, straightforward manner. School administrators have suffered in the public's esteem because of an inability to state succinctly and articulately the ethical aspects of teaching and learning. The Potter's box is one step toward providing a solution for this particular leadership problem.

SUMMARY

Ethical and moral leadership is synonymous with good leadership. Although in the past, leaders were able to skirt the edges of ethical requirements, such is no longer the case for long-term leadership. At the same time, leaders can no longer sit on the fence on many ethical decisions; their constituents demand an honest position. Ethical decision making is key to good leadership, but moral principles may conflict. The Potter's box is a tool for demonstrating moral principles and problems in terms of facts, values, and loyalties.

FIVE FAST FUNDAMENTALS FROM THIS CHAPTER

1. Ethical leadership is an important component of good leadership and articulating ethical principles an important leadership skill.
2. Constituents want honesty as much as any other quality in their leaders.
3. Trust is a powerful emotion that can be tapped to enhance leadership.
4. Schools have become a forum for ethical controversies and school leaders must act accordingly.
5. The Potter's box provides a straightforward heuristic process for ethical analysis.

CHAPTER 7

Diversity Leadership: Dissecting an Emotionally Charged Issue

The issue of diversity has been treated extensively by many writers and theorists. We approach the subject with great trepidation. Many of the finest thinkers of our time have labored to find ways to bring us together and promote harmony and good will among different groups. What can we add to the mix? Some school leaders say they are unhappy with much of the writing on the subject because it offers very little practical direction for the school leaders dealing with diversity issues. Our approach will be, as in previous chapters, to provide practical guidance based in the latest research about human nature and the emotions. Perhaps our discussion on this subject should begin with findings from the highly publicized Human Genome Project. Researchers in the National Genome Research Center and Celara Genomics, the two competing teams on the project, found no set of genes that correspond to racial or ethnic identities. The *New York Times* (Mysteries 2001), in an editorial commenting on the Human Genome Project, said the work of the project "reinforced the idea that race and ethnicity are only skin deep" (A16). Craig Vetter, the director of Celera Genomics, stated that "Race has no genetic or scientific basis" (Olson 2001, 69). When one considers the struggle associated with issues of race, this is a stunning observation. The work of these researchers concurs with earlier findings that the make-up of all human kind is basically the same. Although we may look different on the outside, genetically the differences are minimal. If the categorizations used most often to divide us (race and ethnicity) are not based in scientific reality but derived from superficial observation, what is real and what is subjective interpretation in our beliefs about people? The biologist E. O. Wilson (1998) described the ongoing genetic and biological research in his book, *Consilience*. "We are a single gene pool from which individuals are drawn in each generation and into which they are dissolved in the next generation, forever united as a species by heritage and common future. Such are the conceptions, based on fact, from which new intimations of immortality can be drawn and a mythos evolved." By invoking our common heritage and future as human beings on planet Earth, Wilson describes bonds that unite all of us. These bonds are much stronger than any differences we perceive or should be willing to accept.

Maybe the term *diversity initiative* is not the best label for efforts to unify us. Given the similarity of our genetic structure, perhaps we would be wise to emphasize our similarities instead of our differences. *Unity initiative* might be a better way to describe our efforts to work together and develop an appreciation for the contribution that every single individual can make to a school. In the remainder of this chapter, we continue to use the term *diversity* because of the wide usage and understanding associated with the term. The work on diversity that we cite promotes a mind-set that seeks to emphasize our common bonds and minimize our differences.

Emotionally, we all react to loss with sadness. We all welcome the experience of happiness and love. We are all bound together by our shared humanity. Where we differ is in our perceptions and interpretations of reality. Our perceptions of what we experience are very different because our emotions filter out unnecessary input from our environment and provide us with only the information we need to survive and thrive. We are deluged with a constant stream of perceptions, images, and other sensory experiences. In order to avoid being overwhelmed by all of this neural raw material, the emotions filter out some of this sensory information and focus on the input deemed necessary for the moment. The neurologist Donald Caine (1999) stated that we perceive only (a) what is biologically important, (b) what we look for, and (c) what we have been trained to see. Our perceptions are filtered through subjective emotional filters, providing us with a subjective perception of reality. Our perceptions are subjective and dependent on our emotions. All school leaders should be aware of our neurological predisposition for subjectivity. Leadership subjectivity is a particularly important consideration when working with diversity issues.

A POSITIVE MIND-SET TOWARD DIVERSITY

Leadership and Subjectivity

Leaders must know themselves. Knowing that we are not hardwired to be objective is important self-knowledge for any educational leader. We all have certain biases and we see things in schools in different ways. The effective leader realizes his preconceptions, whether religious, ethnic, or socioeconomic. Knowing our own biases is an important first step before implementing a school or school system diversity initiative. Leaders must examine their own prejudices before advocating inclusion for the rest of the school community. By acknowledging biases and working to mitigate their effects, the leader can model an important aspect of celebrating diversity. Awareness of the human penchant for subjectivity can also aid the leader as she works to stay in tune with the emotional dispositions of constituents. Leaders should work to see things from the subjective perspective of constituents. Acceptance of the subjective nature of perception and a willingness to attempt to see things the way others see them will be of particular help to the leader in the interpersonal skills of persuasion, motivation, conflict resolution, and communication.

Using Evaluation to Demonstrate a Commitment to Diversity

Given the human proclivity for subjectivity, the evaluation process can be used to promote a positive attitude to diversity. Evaluation is a critical function of leadership. The school leader can demonstrate a genuine respect for an inclusive perspective through the use of 360-degree feedback. This 360-degree feedback provides for many different constituents to be involved in evaluation. For example, in a 360-degree evaluation of the principal, the principal would not only be evaluated by his superior (for example, the superintendent or associate superintendent), he would also be assessed by selected peers (other principals), and representative teachers, parents, students, noncertificated educators, and other designated constituents. Each evaluator would provide an assessment from his or her unique perspective. This type of evaluation gives powerful evidence of the leader's respect for a wide spectrum of opinions and viewpoints. The process itself illustrates the leader's embrace of diversity in an extremely important area of leadership. The inclusion of varied viewpoints in the evaluation process sets a positive tone for engaging issues of diversity.

Creating a Favorable Environment for Diversity

It is obvious leaders should use their leadership skills to create an environment that fosters a welcoming attitude toward differences in the school setting. Less obvious are specific strategies to create the desired mind-set in school constituents. We believe that conflict management offers an important opportunity for leaders to demonstrate their commitment to diversity. Every day school leaders must settle a variety of disputes. Leaders at all levels of school leadership, from superintendents to assistant principals, can use the process of conflict resolution to demonstrate sincerity in their attitudes toward diversity. The conflict resolution style adopted by the school leader affords an opportunity for the leader to demonstrate a commitment to working with different perspectives. Morgan (1997) proposes five styles for dealing with conflict in organizations that are characterized by the following behaviors:

1. Avoiding: The leader ignores conflict and hopes it will go away.
2. Compromise: The leader asks each side to give up something in order to gain something they value.
3. Competition: The leader creates a situation in which one side wins everything and one side loses everything.
4. Accommodation: The leader asks one side to give way and not allow a conflict to develop.
5. Collaboration: The leader facilitates problem solving by asking each side to confront differences and share ideas. Both sides attempt to find solutions where both sides can win.

We believe the collaborative approach to conflict management can assist in creating a positive environment for diversity. The collaborative style causes both sides to understand the other side's position. This approach creates an environment in which differences must first be understood and then become part of the solution to the problem. In adopting this style of conflict resolution, the school leader demonstrates that engaging differences is an integral part of the exercise of school leadership.

The preceding section, described ways in which the school leader can create an environment that will be favorable for promoting inclusion and fostering a positive mind-set toward diversity. The remainder of this chapter describes strategies for initiating formal training in diversity.

DIVERSITY INITIATIVES

Establishing Ground Rules for a Formal Diversity Initiative

The first decision to be made before implementing diversity training is to determine whether participation will be mandatory or voluntary. We strongly urge that all diversity training be conducted on a voluntary basis. Personnel may be encouraged to participate but they must not be compelled to be involved in any training. Many diversity programs have been irreparably damaged because people were coerced to participate. The leadership skill of persuasion once again comes into play here. Educational leaders from superintendents to principals should use their persuasive skills to show constituents the value of diversity training but they must not mandate participation. Perhaps part of the persuasive effort would be a discussion of the Human Genome Project. This approach is consistent with all we have said about the emotions and motivation. If constituents are to be motivated to examine their core beliefs and change their behavior, they must do so based upon their genuine emotional drives and motivation. Cherniss (2000) described the difference between cognitive and emotional learning. In cognitive learning, new information is added to existing neurological categories; in emotional learning, existing neural pathways must be altered or extinguished before changes in behavior can take place. In order for emotional learning to take place, the learner must be committed and willing to allow old neural patterns to be eliminated. This demands voluntary engagement. Diversity training, because it involves deeply held core beliefs, requires emotional learning.

Determining the Initial Focus for a Diversity Program

Once voluntary guidelines for participation in the diversity program have been established, consideration should be given to the initial focus for training. Hayles and Mendez-Russell (1997) recommend a broad focus in the initial phase of diversity training. A broadly focused program would involve considering many kinds of differences rather than a specific focus on race or gender. Participants in the diversity training would be asked to consider how all kinds of differences affect us, such as political, religious, cultural, and physical, along with race and gender. The training facilitator can then note that even with all these differences, we still have many similarities. This broad approach should foster a feeling of inclusion on the part of participants that will advance the training effort. A more narrowly gauged approach that centers on race or gender could create feelings of exclusion in the participants. By recognizing that we are all different in many ways and similar in many other ways, perspectives can be developed in participants that eventually lead to inclusive ways of perceiving the school setting. If a more narrow focus is taken at the initial stage of the program, some participants might feel excluded and even resentful, and at this point, emotional learning cannot take place.

Models for Diversity Training

Once voluntary guidelines for participation are instituted and a broad focus for the program is formulated, the model for the diversity training should be selected. Hayles and Mendez-Russell (1997) described several models for group and individual development. This section summarizes two of those models.

The Bennett Model

The Bennett Model, created by Milton J. Bennett, proposes six stages of development in perception, feelings, knowledge, and interpersonal skills in working with difference.

- Stage 1 *Denial of difference*: At this stage, the participant refuses to engage in issues of diversity.

- Stage 2 *Defense against difference*: In this phase, the participant perceives differences in negative terms.
- Stage 3 *Minimization of difference*: At this level, the participant finds it difficult to view people as different and also equal.
- Stage 4 *Acceptance of difference*: At this stage, participants are able to view differences positively.
- Stage 5 *Adaptation to difference*: In this phase, participants perceive differences and are able to successfully adapt to them.
- Stage 6 *Integration of differences*: At this level, participants perceive differences and are able to value differences in the school setting.

Bennett recommends specific interventions and strategies to enable participants to overcome biases and move to higher levels of perception, feelings, knowledge, and behavior at each stage.

The Mendez-Russell Model

This model, formulated by Armida Mendez-Russell, envisions four categories of development within each category of development, and two areas for exploration of perception, feelings, knowledge, and interpersonal skills in working with diversity. The model can be illustrated in the following manner:

Categories	**Deeper Exploration**
Knowledge (Head)	Move from Stereotype To Factual Information
Understanding (Heart)	Move from Awareness To Empathy
Acceptance (Hand and Heart)	Move from Tolerance To Respect
Behavior (Hand and Heart)	Move from Self-Awareness To Exercising Interpersonal Skills

Participants in programs based on this model would move within a specific category to deeper levels of exploration to advance their perceptions, knowledge, feelings, and behavior to higher levels. For example, within the category of behavior, school personnel would participate in interventions that would aid them in progressing from being aware of the value of working in a diverse environment (self-awareness) to gaining skills in communication, persuasion, conflict resolution, and networking (interpersonal skills) in a diverse school community.

SUMMARY

In this chapter, we have described strategies that can lead to the creation of an environment conducive to embracing diversity in the school setting. Among these strategies are the use of the 360-degree feedback process and a collaborative style of conflict management. We have discussed several models for formal diversity initiatives and described parameters and ground rules for the initiation of those diversity models. Perhaps most importantly, we have emphasized research on the human propensity for subjective perception and cautioned school leaders to acknowledge this behavioral trait and factor it into their preparation for engaging diversity issues.

FIVE FAST FUNDAMENTALS FROM THIS CHAPTER

1. The leader's approach to evaluation and conflict management can aid the success of a diversity initiative.
2. Leaders should accept the fact that they are subjective and use this knowledge in the exercise of leadership.
3. Participation in formal diversity training should be on a voluntary basis.
4. Formal diversity training should focus on a variety of differences and not focus exclusively on gender or race.
5. The objective of an emphasis on diversity should be an appreciation of difference by all members of the school community.

CHAPTER 8

School Culture, Emotions, and Leadership

School culture can be described as the aggregate set of beliefs, values, attitudes, moral principles, behaviors, and emotions that are prevalent in a school and school system. The school culture encompasses the entire array of educational practices within an educational institution, both formal and informal, both approved and nonapproved. A discussion of school culture allows us to sum up all we have discussed in the preceding chapters because the culture of the school is the ultimate result of the three ingredients we contend are the most important in exercising school leadership: the leader, the constituents, and the situation.

The interaction of these three elements creates the school culture. We further contend that education cultures are unique in their leadership requirements. All leaders must work with people. The practice of school leadership involves working with people not only as constituents but as raw materials (people who need to learn and be taught) and as product (people who have received an education). School leadership is conducted in an especially people-rich environment. This makes school leadership different from leadership in the business world and more akin to politics or government, also conducted in people-rich environments. A recent *New York Times* story about difficulties encountered by the chancellor of the New York public school system illustrates our point:

> With each new stumbling block, Mr. Levy is learning that the school system, with its many fiefs and interest groups, byzantine politics and influence peddlers, bears no resemblance to the corporate world. Instead of a

> hierarchical company in which the boss calls all the shots, he is facing a system with myriad constituencies, all of whom help run it and expect a say in decisions large and small. Many in that system have bridled at Mr. Levy's top-down style, which they describe as blunt and imperious. "Harold's a businessman, and once he decides that this is the way to do something, it's hard to sway him off that course," said Ernest Clayton, president of the United Parents Associations of New York City. "But he's not dealing with widgets anymore. He's dealing with people, and he needs to collaborate." (Goodnough 2001, B3)

Harold Levy, chancellor of the New York school system, certainly faced a daunting task in working with the particular culture of New York City. However, despite the size and complexity of New York, the problems he experienced are not unique. Certainly, the reaction to his leadership is familiar to almost anyone who has tried to run a school system. At a crucial point in their careers, most superintendents will be reminded that they are in a people enterprise. As the representative for the parents' association so eloquently says in the article, school superintendents are not making widgets. School superintendents must deal with people.

As we stated in the very first paragraph of the book, the primary focus of school leadership is people, and the primary purpose of school leadership is to work with people in a productive manner. This reality is the first thing school leaders need to remember when working to nurture a learner-centered school culture. While keeping the constituents in the culture paramount, we believe that restoring educators' pride in their profession is extremely important in fostering a culture that will be conducive to the best possible learning environment for students.

FOSTERING SCHOOL CULTURE

Pride in Our Profession

The Basques are a people group who live in northern Spain. We have been told that people in that province take particular pride in their profession, whatever it is. If a Basque bricklayer is asked who is the best bricklayer in town, he will say, "For me, I am the best." This expression of pride in one's work is not considered boastful or a type of bragging, rather it is simply a way to say that I work very hard at what I do because what I do is important and should be done in the right manner. People need good bricklayers; it is important work and if it is not done correctly, there are very bad consequences. We believe we must nurture this type of culture in our schools.

Superintendents must constantly remind everyone connected with education that they are doing very important work and that it should be done well. If it is done well, our whole society is made better. Superintendents should make opportunities to say this frequently, not only to educators but also to all the constituencies with whom they interact. Pride in our work touches strong emotions and gives meaning and purpose to our lives. This meaning and purpose is the reason that most of us chose education as a career. School leaders must help to keep those emotions burning strong and bright in their constituents. If educators do not take pride in their profession, who will?

Instruction and Learning

As stated in the chapter on instructional leadership, student achievement is the standard by which school leaders will be measured. It is therefore important for school leaders to encourage the development of a culture that makes instruction and learning paramount within the school environment. The school leader, whether at the building or system level, must make it clear that the instructional program is the top priority. Instruction and learning are the key situational elements as the educational leader analyzes the school culture.

The school leader can sometimes demonstrate the importance of teaching through the use of symbolic leadership. Symbolic leadership is the use of emotionally charged symbols or actions to touch deep feelings in constituents and to explicitly depict the leader's and the institution's commitment to a cause. When a principal or superintendent takes the opportunity to substitute for a teacher in the classroom, it is an important symbolic gesture. This gesture is a way of saying that the principal or superintendent believes that teaching is of the utmost importance and the value of what the classroom teacher does has not been forgotten in the press of other leadership demands. Spending time in the classroom also gains credibility for the school leader by demonstrating that the leader still knows what instruction is all about. Frequent stints in the classroom also keep the leader aware of the difficulties and problems faced by the classroom teacher.

Honoring the Profession

Awards for teaching and instructional design are another example of symbolic leadership. If the award is of little value or the award ceremony is conducted in a perfunctory manner, then the symbolic message is that teaching is not valued in this culture. Therefore, it is important that teaching or instructional design awards meet certain standards.

1. Awards should have respectable value. Leaders should seek help from business constituents in presenting an award that has real monetary value. In our society, value is often synonymous with monetary value. The symbolic power of the award is lost if the award is perceived as lacking worth.
2. Awards should not be tainted by politics or favoritism. Superintendents should personally intervene to ensure that the award process is fair and based on merit. It is better to make no award than to allow individuals to receive an award because it was *their department's turn* or *they had an "in" with the judges*. This type of behavior not only demeans the award, it demeans the education profession. The primary purpose of the award ceremony is to honor the profession.
3. Awards should be presented with dignity and proper ceremony. Every administrator and board member should attend the award ceremony in the school system. The ceremony should be held in a location suitable to honoring the profession.

The Emotional Price of Teacher Dismissal

The dismissal of employees is sometimes necessary to achieve or maintain quality in the instructional program. The dismissal of teachers is a highly emotional situation for an educational leader but the strong emotional content of this situation is rarely acknowledged. Many papers have been written about the high cost of teacher dismissal in terms of dollar amounts and the need for voluminous documentation. Little has been written about the wrenching emotional cost to both the employee and the administrator when dismissal is necessary.

Principals, in interviews with educational leadership preparation students, said that the most difficult part of the process of teacher dismissal was not the documentation requirements or the time and money involved, but the emotional energy expended not only by administrators and the person being dismissed but also by other constituents, such as friends of the dismissed teacher. Some principals, when allowed to speak anonymously, said the process was so emotionally draining that they have avoided getting involved in another dismissal procedure. These principals have opted instead to transfer incompetent teachers to other schools.

The legal and technical aspects of dismissal are important but they have been treated extensively in other venues. Our purpose here is to point out the emotional aspect of dismissal and the impact of this emotional cost on the culture of schools. We have ignored in the professional literature the emotional havoc caused by the extreme administrative action of firing personnel. One result, we believe, is that leaders who have responsibility for initiating dismissal actions sometimes avoid the dismissal process. When dismissal is warranted, it is injurious to the instructional program to avoid it. This has a pernicious effect on school culture. It undermines the leader's effort to make instruction and learning paramount within the culture of the school. Instead, it establishes the perception of a leadership compromise with mediocrity or incompetence. The first step to correct this situation is to acknowledge that the dismissal procedure is not only damaging to the person being dismissed but is also emotionally wrenching for the school leader initiating the action. It involves the loss of a member of the school family. It involves judgments about the worth of other human beings and the possible loss of livelihood for that human being because of those judgments. It requires the expenditure of huge amounts of emotional energy. We should be aware of this as school leaders and provide not only technical assistance but also emotional aid in the form of support and empathetic listeners to leaders involved in the dismissal process.

Toward an Emotionally Intelligent School Culture

The old verities about leadership are often true. We should model the leadership behaviors we believe to be essential. We should practice what we preach. Toward that end, the following is a listing of leadership behaviors that, if practiced by the leader and adopted by constituents, will create a culture that is emotionally aware and helpful in managing emotions and relationships.

1. Listen more than you speak. The key communication skill for the modern school leader is listening ability. The following persuasive abilities are predicated on the ability to actively listen to constituents' concerns and base your persuasion on the needs and desires you have heard.
2. Use persuasion rather than coercion whenever possible. Although coercion may work for the immediate situation, Newton's law that for every action there is an equal and opposite reaction holds for coercive leadership. Coercive tactics are eventually countered with opposing coercive tactics and all parties to the contest suffer. On the other hand, even an unsuccessful effort to persuade is usually applauded. "At least she took the time to explain what she is going to try to do," constituents often say. Persuasion almost always has a favorable effect upon those who are being persuaded.
3. Encourage problem-solving conflict resolution. Make each party to a dispute part of the solution to the dispute. Encourage each side to understand the other side and to provide win–win solutions.
4. Network with all constituencies. Keep in touch with all constituencies involved in the enterprise of schooling. Although it is time consuming, it brings big dividends in good relations and information.
5. Participative decision making should be used whenever possible. We once asked a group of principals what site-based management meant to them and one responded, "The teachers come to the site, and I manage them." The teachers with whom we work will no longer accept that leadership style. With great expenditures of energy and emotion, a principal can impose that style of leadership. Modern-day educators, however, will simply not give their best efforts under those leadership conditions.

SUMMARY

Schools cannot operate without the support of constituents, and good leaders remember to gain the support of their teachers through persuasion rather than coercive techniques. A school's culture is a representation of the leader's style, the situation, and the constituents. Sincerely supporting the constituents (the teachers) is essential to good leadership, and we have listed a number of ways to do this.

FIVE FAST FUNDAMENTALS FROM THIS CHAPTER

1. School culture can be described as the aggregate set of beliefs, values, attitudes, moral principles, behaviors, and emotions that are prevalent in a school and school system.
2. Superintendents must constantly remind everyone connected with education that they are doing very important work and that it should be done well.
3. It is important for school leaders to encourage the development of a culture that makes instruction and learning paramount within the school environment.
4. Symbolic leadership is the use of emotionally charged symbols or actions to touch deep feelings in constituents and to explicitly depict the leader's and the institution's commitment to a cause.
5. There is an emotional aspect to dismissal and this aspect impacts the culture of the school.

CHAPTER 9

Managing the Emotions of Change

Change, once the exception, is now the rule in education. Historically, educational change has come with a high price tag and has followed long periods of resistance in which many promising initiatives fell victim to ineffective leadership and passive-aggressive constituents. With the new millennium came renewed calls for school change spawned by a wave of change throughout society. Among the changes affecting education most significantly was the expectation that schools be lead by individuals well versed in instruction. That expectation was closely followed by the expectation that schools also be lead by individuals who know how to bring about changes that will produce improved teaching and learning. This linkage between instructional leadership and change leadership is reflected in the standards for school leaders discussed in earlier chapters. This chapter reviews the impact of emotional intelligence on a school leader's ability to effectively manage the change process. Our focus is on applying what is known about change to the key elements we introduced earlier and to emotional intelligence.

THE NATURE OF CHANGE

Many books have been written about change. Most of those books address change in the business world and can be helpful to school leaders interested in better understanding the change process, but schools cannot be led or changed in exactly the same manner as a business can be led or changed. Yet school leaders are often told they should emulate the behaviors of business leaders. There is no doubt that many of the characteristics of effective leadership are generic. By that, we mean the skills that make leaders successful in one situation, environment, or organization could well be useful in others. What is often forgotten, however, is that success in one environment does not ensure success in another. Even though leaders bring with them all the skills that enabled them to succeed in one organization, they must adjust to a new organization based on the constituents and organizational culture of the new organization. Success in making that adjustment requires knowledge of the new organization and the nature of its business. Our focus is on change leadership in the school. We have taken the essential principles from the change literature and applied them to the school setting. Of all the books written on change, *Managing Transitions* by William Bridges has been the most influential on our work. We recommend it for further reading on change.

Change is really quite simple. It consists of stopping one thing and starting something new. Change typically produces few complications when applied to inanimate objects. Changing the font on a computer or changing the oil in an automobile produces few complications for human or machine. Change becomes complex when human beings are involved. Part of the reason is that change is accompanied by psychological transitions. Psychological transitions are the changes that must occur in the heads of the people whose lives are affected. These psychological transitions are rife with emotion and will ultimately dictate the success or failure of a change initiative. Leaders who understand the psychological transitions that accompany change are much better equipped to successfully change their schools.

Psychological Transitions

Schools are notoriously resistant to change. By this, we mean schools rarely complete the change process. The reason for this is that educators rarely complete the psychological transitions necessary for change to be fully integrated into the school's standard operating procedures. Without that vital step, change is temporary at best. Transition is difficult because it requires letting go of old realities and identities. That might not sound like a very big deal, but the psychological realities associated with reality and identity must be considered. The mind is a powerful and wonderful organ. It allows individuals to make sense of the world around them. The realities it creates influence the analysis of data; what is already known influences the interpretation of what is yet to be known.

The realities associated with work and organizations serve the same purpose. Changes in an organization require changes in reality. Even more complex are changes that affect identity. Changes are typically perceived as threats to the identities individuals in an organization have developed. Identity is essential because it makes people feel comfortable when they know their place in the organization. They know who they are and how they fit. That comfort is very important. This fact is made abundantly clear when we recall situations in which people have resisted changes that would make their jobs easier, result in greater success for them and the organization, and improve their status within the organization.

Psychological transition has been compared to death. This analogy is useful for leaders who want to bring real change to their schools. The analogy reveals the depth of feelings people experience when dealing with psychological transitions. Simply stated, old realities and old identities must die before new realities and new identities can be established. Leaders are not immune to the psychological transitions associated with change. Understanding the process and the realities associated with change can help leaders more effectively deal with their own feelings and emotions. Even more important, understanding psychological transitions is vital for leaders who are assisting other members of the organization deal with change.

Dealing with Psychological Transitions

Just knowing that all members of an organization must complete psychological transitions in order for change efforts to succeed is not enough. Effective leaders use this knowledge along with proven techniques to make lasting changes in their schools. As changes are being planned, specific consideration of the steps required to identify perceived losses and assist individuals with their transitions significantly improve a leader's chances of success. As we stated in chapter 5, real change creates a sense of loss. Leaders must nurture a culture that helps constituents deal with that loss.

Steps needed to identify losses are:

- Envision the new reality that will follow the change. Carefully compare the new reality with the old reality. Identify exactly how the school will be different. This information will make it possible to determine who will lose and what loss they will perceive.
- Anticipate the secondary changes that will accompany a primary change initiative. These secondary changes resemble the ripples that spread across the smooth surface of a pond when a pebble is thrown into the water. If unanticipated, these secondary changes will significantly affect the desired new reality.
- Determine how the information gleaned from the analysis of old realities versus new realities and the information gleaned from the analysis of secondary changes can be used to determine how individuals in the school will perceive potential loss. Once completed, this list will likely include emotion-laded entries like loss of an established routine, loss of a sense of competence, and loss of opportunities to work with colleagues with whom a relationship has already been established.
- Determine exactly what will end as a result of the change. This is related to loss, but we are talking about more than perception. Think about what the new reality will actually mean for every member of the organization.

PLANNING FOR CHANGE AND TRANSITIONS

The following account shows what can happen when a school leader introduces change without planning for the psychological transitions that accompany change. It is a story that we have modified only slightly to demonstrate how important planning for transition really is.

Helen Fisher has just been appointed the new principal of a small elementary school. This is her first principalship and she is eager to do a good job. As an assistant principal, she felt that her principal should have been a much better instructional leader and she was determined to be the kind of leader he should have been. The former principal of the school was well known for a parent outreach program he had started. The program won state and national recognition for involving low socioeconomic parents in school activities. Upon being selected as the new principal, Helen was called into the superintendent's office and told she must do something to raise the school's reading scores. This was the kind of assignment Helen had wanted. She would get the opportunity to make some changes to improve teaching and learning. She searched for the most effective program for improving reading in schools like hers. The one she selected had very impressive data supporting its effectiveness and required little teacher training. As a matter of fact, the new program came with support materials that, if administered properly, ensured positive results.

At her first meeting with the teachers, Helen talked about how much she wanted to build on the achievements of the school and its fine staff. She talked about how important she felt it was to work as a team. She told the staff that she wanted them to be involved in decision making at the school. She then presented some data on the student's reading performance and asked if reading was a problem they needed to address. The staff was impressed by the skills Helen displayed and knew from her reputation as an assistant that they were fortunate to have her as their new principal. Helen sensed that her new colleagues were impressed. Because the meeting was so positive and going so well, Helen decided to mention the program she had discovered to improve reading skills. The staff immediately accepted Helen's suggestion that they try the program. Prior to Helen's arrival, the teachers had discussed their frustrations with the reading program they were using and were growing weary of the time and energy being devoted to the parent involvement program. Seeing the energy and excitement she had generated, Helen quickly sent several teachers to visit schools using the program and when they returned with glowing reports, she announced that the program would be purchased and implemented immediately.

Helen then devoted herself to making the new program a success. She worked tirelessly to make sure teachers and students had the support they needed. She did not think it was necessary to make any plans or take any action to help the staff deal with the change to the new program. After all, the staff had embraced the new program and had clearly seen the need to improve the student's reading skills. Why should she waste her time and energy dealing with a nonissue?

Helen did not see the first signs that psychological transitions were causing problems for the staff. Her assumptions that everyone shared her enthusiasm for the new program and determination not to let minor problems derail the initiative resulted in growing isolation from the staff. It was not until a group of teachers came to her to talk about their concern that parents no longer felt welcomed in the school that she began to see that things were not as she had thought.

By the time Helen took the time to assess the situation, she discovered the following:

- The teachers felt the new program limited their flexibility and was professionally demeaning. (They were uncomfortable with the new teaching procedures.)
- Those staff members who had been active supporters of the parent involvement program and perceived as leaders of that program were complaining about parents being pushed out of the school. (They perceived the new program as causing them to lose power.)
- The new program had resulted in significant changes in the school schedule that the teachers felt interfered with student learning. (They were uncomfortable with new routines and wanted the security that comes with familiar procedures.)

Could Planning Have Helped?

Helen has a problem that a little planning and monitoring could have helped her address before it became well established. She demonstrated high skill as a problem analyzer and could have used that skill to identify how the school would change once the new reading program was initiated. This would have made her aware of the potential for problems associated with asking teachers to use a new technique.

She would have been well served if she had spent some time thinking about the secondary changes that would occur. The secondary changes included less emphasis for the parent involvement program. Helen never intended to stop the parent involvement program, but there is only so much time and energy available in any school and the new program required lots of both. She should have realized that it would.

Helen felt that the general initial enthusiasm for the program meant everyone was as dedicated to its success as she was. After all, she was dealing with major changes herself. If she were willing to minimize her need to deal with the psychological transitions she felt that resulted from assuming a new position, surely her new constituents would be willing to put the new program ahead of their transitions needs.

She should have realized the not everyone would share her commitment and that dealing with these needs would be part of making the change to the new program complete. Finally, no thought was given to losses the staff would perceive. Had Helen made this part of her planning process, she might have been able to anticipate and effectively deal with them before they jeopardized the program's success.

What Happens When It's Too Late to Plan

Helen is well into the change in the reading program and now realizes she should have planned for the psychological transitions the staff is experiencing. She can still deal effectively with the situation. To do so, she must gather information and deal with the issues the transitions have created. She must do the following:

- Listen without arguing or making constituents feel they are not understood.
- Expect constituents to overreact. Emotions are not connected to logic during the initial stages of change.
- Expect to have to deal with emotions connected to prior ineffective change efforts. If constituents have not effectively moved through the psychological transitions spawned by prior change initiatives, they could vent frustrations they harbor during subsequent periods of change.
- Prepare constituents to view the change initiative as the first step in a series of changes that will affect them in significant ways.
- Bring losses and perceived losses into the open and prepare to deal with them honestly and with genuine concern.

THE EMOTIONS OF TRANSITIONS

Because change includes the death of the old followed by rebirth of the new, it is not surprising that many of the emotions associated with change are like the emotions associated with a death. Leaders need to understand the emotions of the change process for many reasons. Understanding leads to sincere empathy and a more patient approach to helping constituents work through their transitions. Leaders who do not anticipate emotional reactions to change might think constituents are just being difficult or uncooperative. They might also decide that they have heard enough griping and stop listening. If they do these things, the transitions stop and successful change is the casualty. It is impossible to predict the precise emotions that constituents will experience during change, but leaders and their constituents often experience the following:

- Anger in its full range, from passive-aggressive behavior to rage
- Anxiety that seems unrealistic
- Sadness that ranges from silence to crying
- Shell shock that results in confusion or disorientation
- Depression ranging from just being down to severe hopelessness

To help constituents and themselves deal with these emotions, leaders should listen, listen, listen, and then listen more. Listening should not be associated with approving or accepting blame for the distress. Listening does not mean accepting verbal abuse. Listening includes being open to suggestions that additional changes be made and to suggestions that returning to *some* of the old ways is necessary. It does not include always agreeing with these suggestions. One of the most difficult tasks a leader faces is knowing when to stay the course and when to move to plan B. There is no secret formula we can offer for making that decision. We do know that listening to a wide range of individuals and not rushing to judgment will help. Another benefit leaders derive from listening is that often it is all constituents want—someone to listen and commiserate. It can also be therapeutic for leaders who, by listening to others, are entitled to express their feelings.

Emotional intelligence is most helpful in situations in which leaders can use their understanding of the emotions others feel to be more effective. During the change process, this understanding pays huge dividends.

After a Change

One would expect something positive to happen immediately following a change. After all, change results from efforts to make things better. Research, unfortunately, has clearly shown that things get worse following the initiation of change. This phenomenon has many names. We call it the implementation dip. It is that period of indecision and confusion that naturally occurs when constituents and leaders are expected to stop functioning as they have and are told to function in a different way. The implementation dip can cause leaders to question their judgment and grow frustrated. It can cause teachers even more frustration and produce emotional reactions. If the implementation dip is successfully traversed, the organization will move back to the prechange level of performance and then to a higher level of performance than was possible under the old realities.

The implementation dip is an important period for leaders. During this period, no one is happy, the brain is dominated by emotion, and cognition occurs through an emotional filter. During this period, leaders play key roles that will ultimately determine the success of the change initiative.

Keys to Leader Behavior in the Dip

- Constituents are feeling loss. Find ways to compensate them.
- Communicate, communicate, communicate, and never assume constituents understand the situation as leaders do. Check for understanding.
- Make sure everyone understands what to stop doing. People will not stop doing the old things at the same time they implement the new until they burn out or understand they are to stop.
- Be sure to talk about the old realities with respect. People generally do the best work they know how to do. Change suggests that old ways were not good enough. Effective leaders take care to respect old realities and put them in perspective.
- Honor the past by making it the foundation upon which the new reality is being built.
- Initiating change is easy. The difficult task is to motivate and support constituents as they make the psychological transition to the new reality.

CHANGE AND SITUATIONS

We called your attention to the impact situations have on leaders in an earlier chapter. So how do situations affect change leadership? Obviously, to prepare for the impact change will have on a school, two situations must be clearly understood: the situation that existed prior to change and the situation that change will create. Leaders who carefully analyze the prechange situation are able to plan effectively. The envisioned postchange situation enables school leaders to identify how the school will be different. Understanding these two situations will:

- Enable the comparison of the new reality with the old.
- State exactly how the school will be different.
- Determine what losses will occur.
- Predict secondary changes.
- Perceive potential constituent losses.
- Determine what must end as a result of the change.

Another aspect of the current situation that merits consideration is the change tolerance level. The change tolerance level can be determined by evaluating how much additional change constituents will tolerate. This is an important consideration for school leaders in schools that are undergoing numerous local and state reform initiatives. In low change-tolerant schools, leaders must work hard to help constituents see the connections between change initiatives and to provide extra support for constituents. In this situation, leaders must work to limit the volume of change affecting constituents.

In an atmosphere of change, emotional intelligence increases the school leader's awareness of the emotional impact of change. From that knowledge base, a school leader is much more apt to accurately read signals, know when constituents need extra support, and effectively deal with personal stress. The ability to deal with personal stress is a vital component in this mix. Leaders who are unable to deal with their own change emotions are limited in their ability to assist others.

Change and Constituents

In the final analysis, the success of any change will depend on how well constituents accept it and contribute to its success. Even if the change will make their work more effective or easier, constituents will be uncomfortable until they work their way through the initial stages of doing things differently and move through psychological transitions. Emotions will play a significant role in the lives of constituents during periods of change. The emotions will limit their ability to rationally deal with the situation at hand. Emotions will surface in a variety of ways and at different times.

The keys for school leaders dealing with constituents during periods of change are the following:

- Anticipate the impact changes will have on constituents.
- Plan to deal with anticipated emotional reactions.
- Monitor to determine if the anticipated emotional impact is accurate.
- Support constituents as they make psychological transitions.
- Listen openly to feelings of frustration and suggestions.

Constituents are the most significant element in school change. If constituents do not successfully transition from the old to the new, nothing will change and the potential for improving the quality of teaching and learning will be lost.

Change and Self

School leaders perceive their schools from a perspective that differs from that of other members of the school community. Teachers are focused on their classrooms. Parents are focused on the success of their children. Other members of the school community focus on still other aspects of the school. It is the school leader who must focus on the entire school and balance its conflicting needs. During times of change, this difference in perception becomes a factor that school leaders should consider. The school leader's perception of the need for change, the realities that make one innovation more likely to succeed than another, and vision of a more effective school after the innovation are unknown unless the leader effectively communicates them.

The Passion of Change

Passion is a part of every significant event in history. Passion is a key element in successful change. Often the passion that drives successful change efforts begins with the school leader. That passion must be transferred to other members of the school community if change efforts are to succeed. The transfer of the passion for making the school better must occur in order for change efforts to succeed. Passion can also hinder a school leader's effort to change a school. If not managed properly, a leader's passion can be blinding. Caution must be exercised to ensure that passion does not skew perception and cause leaders to loose sight of the fact that visions must be shared.

Leadership Skills and Change

Many skills are needed to implement change. Many school leaders mistakenly think they must be masters of all these skills. What is more important is for leaders to accurately assess their skills and understand how their strengths can be most effectively used, as well as how to compensate for weaknesses. One vital skill to a leader's success is delegation. Through delegation, leaders can utilize the strengths of a wide range of constituents. Done correctly, delegation requires careful consideration of the task to be delegated, the individual best suited for the task, selling the delegation, monitoring, supporting, and feedback. First-time delegations can easily double a leader's workload. They can also pay huge dividends as constituents grow and develop experiences that enable them to assist leaders in ways that help them compensate for their own weaknesses.

The keys that school leaders need to remember when dealing with themselves during periods of change are the following:

- Understand the strengths that enable you to lead the change.
- Understand the weaknesses that limit success.
- Share perceptions with others to increase overall understanding.
- Share the passion.
- Use your understanding of the change process to manage your feelings.
- Increase resources through delegation.

School leaders play a major role in change initiatives. They are important factors in change efforts. It is important to remember, however, that leaders are not alone in their schools. Others also share the responsibility of school success.

SUMMARY

If schools are to improve, changes must be made. Leaders are expected to lead the change process in their schools. As change efforts are begun, many factors come into play. The emotions associated with change are powerful forces. Constituents are likely to resist change even when it is positive. Helping constituents deal with the psychological transitions that accompany change is an important role for leaders. Planning for change increases the chances for success. Understanding the situations in which change takes place is important for leaders. Understanding situations help leaders to better understand constituent's reactions to change. Leaders themselves are factors in school change efforts. The skills they bring to the situation affect their success. It is important for leaders to understand their own strengths and weaknesses. Delegation is an effective means through which leaders can deal with their weaknesses and workload. School improvement is a responsibility that is shared by all members of the school community and the school leader is its steward.

FIVE FAST FUNDAMENTALS FROM THIS CHAPTER

1. All school leaders must deal with change.
2. Change is a difficult process for individuals and organizations.
3. Effective leaders understand the change process and plan carefully when changes are made.
4. Key skills enable leaders to successfully bring about change in their schools.
5. Change does not generally lead to immediate improvement; remember the implementation dip.

CHAPTER 10

EQ: The Missing Ingredient in School Leadership

The concept of Emotional Intelligence (EQ) fills a void in the field of educational leadership theory. For years, school leaders have asked the question, "What does it take to be a successful administrator?" Often, the answer involved some appraisal of academic skills and cognitive intelligence. In fact, judgments of these abilities are still the major prerequisite for admission to school leadership preparation programs. Certainly there is a need for school leaders to have necessary cognitive and academic skills, but these qualities alone do not make successful school leaders. We all know administrators of superb intellect and academic accomplishment who have failed as educational leaders. Books and articles have been written that analyzed the phenomena of highly intelligent leaders who were unable to cope with the demands of leadership (see Further Readings in Leadership Failures). We believe emotional intelligence and the interpersonal skills based on processing emotional knowledge are the missing ingredients in the continuing dilemma of what makes a successful leader. Other disciplines are also analyzing the effect of emotional intelligence on leadership. Fred Greenstein, director of the Woodrow Wilson Research Program in Leadership Studies at Princeton University, calls emotional intelligence the presidential difference in a book about the leadership abilities of Presidents from Franklin Delano Roosevelt to Bill Clinton (*The Presidential Difference* 2000). Greenstein contends that the emotional intelligence displayed by these Presidents has made the difference between successful and unsuccessful presidencies. The interpersonal skills of communication, persuasion, team building, networking, and conflict resolution would appear to be a necessity in any leadership arena. Imagine a well-regarded principal of ten or fifteen years ago. If this administrator had been punctual and accurate in preparing reports, firm and fair in the administration of discipline, beyond reproach in the conduct of his personal life, provided teachers with the material resources to teach, and left everyone alone to do their jobs, he would have been considered a good administrator. Not so today. The administrator we have just described might not survive in today's school environment. Today, school leaders at all levels, from the superintendents to assistant principals, must establish credentials as instructional leaders. They must project a presence that epitomizes the vision upon which the school is based and they must relate on an emotional, personal level to various constituencies. These demands on the modern-day school leader require the leader to tap into emotional reservoirs of pride, caring, and belonging in members of the school community.

INFORMAL ASSESSMENT OF EQ

In the preceding chapters, we described applications of EQ to many functions of school leadership. This chapter describes applications of EQ that can also serve as informal heuristic assessments to assess the effective application of EQ to school leadership. We use our original definition of leadership as the framework for these informal assessments. In chapter 2, we stated that leadership could be defined by (1) the leader, (2) the constituents, and (3) the situation. Informal assessment of EQ in school leadership can begin with these three elements.

Using EQ in Response to Constituents

Educational leaders should continuously assess to determine if their leadership is attuned to the emotional resonance of their constituents. When communicating, does the administrator listen to the emotional undertones of the message as well as the surface message? Does the leader present information in a way that takes into account the emotional impact of the message as well as the logical effect? Does the leader consider the audience in framing communication for constituents? We have stressed that working with people is the essence of leadership. People are driven to action by their emotions. School leaders must stay in touch with the emotional drives of their constituents. Educators must be ready for periods of change in an era of technological and informational innovations. Change brings anxiety and even fear. School leaders should be particularly concerned about the emotional needs of constituents during periods of change.

The Leader, EQ, and Stress

During a recent medical examination, one of the authors mentioned to a doctor that he was working on a book about school leadership. The doctor performing the examination stated that in the last month he had treated five school administrators for physical symptoms related to stress. "You need to teach these people how to take care of themselves in a stressful environment," he said. "Doesn't anybody know how stressful running a school is?" Stress management is another important application of emotion-based skills. Neurological research indicates that brain waves are affected during relaxation exercises and effective relaxation techniques cause positive physiological reactions throughout the body. Blood pressure is lowered, dopamine and other health-promoting hormones are released, and general health is improved. The relentless demands of school administration require the school executive to engage in stress-reducing activities, such as exercise, meditation, gardening, or any other activity that is fun and offers physical regeneration. These activities help to restore emotional balance and assist in maintaining emotional stability. Participating in activities we find pleasurable has been found to be a successful antidote to depression. Processing information about our emotional and physical status, then working to maintain a healthy equilibrium is an important indicator of emotional intelligence. Ignoring this important aspect of leadership is not emotionally intelligent.

Using EQ in Response to Leadership Failures

Industrious, energetic leaders will eventually encounter failure. The only way a leader can avoid failure is by doing nothing. Winston

Churchill once said, "Success is never final but failure is never fatal." This is the perfect mind-set for the modern-day school leader. This attitude captures the necessary emotional outlook as the leader confronts the uncertainties and ambiguities of school leadership. An accurate gauge of whether a leader is employing emotional intelligence is that leader's response to failure. Does a minor setback such as a missed deadline or unhappy encounter with a parent cause lingering unhappiness? Does the displeasure of constituents over a decision the leader believes to be correct cause him a prolonged period of self-doubt? The ability to maintain optimism during setbacks and failures is another key indicator of emotional intelligence. This is not to say we should respond to failure with joy, but we must keep our professional life in perspective. Failure is not a character trait but a specific circumstance. Analysis of the specific factors in a failed leadership effort is necessary to avoid a recurrence. We must not allow ourselves to begin to believe that the setback has anything to do with our inherent abilities. The fact that we sometimes fail does not make us failures. Maintaining a positive attitude is a leadership skill. Pessimism and optimism are contagious.

Monitoring the Emotional Climate

The leader's judgment of which emotions predominate in any situation in which leadership is required is another important indicator of emotional intelligence. Can a tense situation be defused with a little humor or does the occasion call for the leader to adopt a stern demeanor? The administrator's judgment as to which emotions are strongest in a specific situation and how these emotions should be managed provide yet another informal assessment of emotional intelligence. One of the authors witnessed a newly appointed superintendent quickly lose the confidence of his new staff by constantly telling stories about the wonderful school system in which he previously served. He frequently ignored his current staff as they tried to explain the intricacies of his new school system. He misjudged the emotional content of the situation. The staff did not need the emotional solace of knowing the superintendent had worked in a great system in his previous job. Their emotional drive was to discuss the requirements of the current position. When he continually cut off discussion about his new job to reminisce about his old one, he rapidly lost the confidence of his staff. His misjudgment of the emotional climate of the situation ultimately proved to be very costly.

The preceding examples illustrate various informal means to determine how well emotional intelligence is being applied in specific leadership situations. The next section, covers more formal assessments of emotional intelligence.

FORMAL EQ ASSESSMENT

Mayer, Caruso, and Salovey have provided a comprehensive review of the current state of formal Emotional Intelligence (EQ) assessment. As stated earlier, Salovey and Mayer originated the concept of emotional intelligence. Three types of EQ tests are delineated.

- *Self-Report Assessment*: This type of assessment requires the person being assessed to report his appraisal of his emotional abilities by selecting descriptive statements that most accurately depict his perception of his emotional skills.
- *Informant Assessment*: This measure of emotional intelligence offers information about how a person's emotional intelligence is perceived by those who know the person being assessed.
- *Ability Assessment*: This type of EQ test measures the performance of a person on the emotional abilities under scrutiny.

Mayer, Caruso, and Salovey compare these three types of EQ assessments to appraisals of abilities in mathematics. A self-report assessment could be compared to asking someone if they can perform a specific mathematical function, such as multiplication. An informant type of assessment could be compared to asking an acquaintance of someone if that person can multiply. An ability measure would be the same as asking the person to actually perform the mathematical function, in other words, requiring the person to multiply 50 x 7. The mathematical example illustrates why Mayer, Caruso, and Salovey call ability testing the gold standard in EQ assessment. They contend that requiring EQ test-takers to demonstrate emotional abilities is the most valid method of assessment. For example, rather than asking EQ test-takers how well they perceive emotion in others, an ability measure of that skill would show a sad face to the person being assessed and then ask that person if she recognizes the emotion depicted in the sad face.

Examples of the three types of EQ assessment and the designers of the assessments are listed below.

Self-Report EQ Tests: Bar-On Emotional Inventory (Bar-On EQ-i) 1997, designed by Reuvan Bar-On. Reuvan Bar-On is the co-editor of *The Handbook of Emotional Intelligence: Theory, Development, Assessment, and Application at Home, School and in the Workplace*.

Emotional Intelligence Map (EQ Map) 1997, designed by Robert Cooper. Robert Cooper is the co-author of the book *Executive EQ*.

Informant EQ Test: Emotional Competence Inventory (ECI) 1999, designed by Richard E. Boyatzis, Daniel Goleman, and the Hay/McBer training group. Richard Boyatzis is a noted researcher of emotional competencies. Daniel Goleman is the author of the books *Emotional Intelligence* and *Working with Emotional Intelligence*.

Ability EQ Test: Multifactor Emotional Intelligence Scale (MEIS) 1997, designed by John D. Mayer, Peter Salovey, and David R. Caruso. As stated earlier, Mayer and Salovey originated the concept of emotional intelligence.

SUMMARY

In this chapter, we have described both informal and formal means of assessing emotional intelligence. Implicit in this discussion has been the belief that, given the importance of emotional intelligence in the exercise of leadership, some means of assessing EQ should be conducted as part of leadership assessment. Any evaluation measure can be abused or used inappropriately but careful assessment of emotional intelligence should improve the practice of leadership in school systems.

FIVE FAST FUNDAMENTALS FROM THIS CHAPTER

1. The concept of emotional intelligence provides an important missing ingredient to understanding effective school leadership.

2. Informally assessing a leader's response to constituents, stress, and failure can offer valuable insight into the leader's emotional intelligence.
3. Good leaders see failure as a temporary set of circumstances, not a permanent character trait.
4. Ability testing of EQ is the gold standard in EQ assessment.
5. Informal and formal assessments of EQ should be a part of leadership feedback.

Summing Up

In the preceding pages, we have attempted to provide, in the most straightforward manner possible, our thoughts and beliefs about what makes a good school leader. We have tried to support our assertions with the best and most recent research. In condensing these thoughts on school leadership to their most basic, irreducible elements, we have focused on constituents, situations, and you, the school leader.

We have advanced the notion that the most important skills in school leadership are skills employed for interpersonal exchanges. Skills such as listening, persuading, motivating, resolving conflicts, and communicating are the backbone of school leadership and are based in emotional knowledge and direction. We have also promoted the idea that the concept of emotional intelligence is the missing ingredient in the formula for successful leadership. Obviously, leaders need a certain level of basic intelligence and job knowledge. What have been more difficult to pinpoint are the intangible qualities that enable a leader to know and manage his or her emotional stability and engender emotional awareness and assurance in others. We believe the concept of emotional intelligence provides vital insight into these critical skill sets.

During the course of this book, we have also endeavored to provide a real-world context and framework for discussions about leadership and emotional intelligence. We have tried to place our explanations of the research and concepts in the nitty-gritty environment in which school leadership occurs. Clearly, we believe the road to good leadership is a journey, not a fixed destination. We hope we have been of some service to you as you have traveled along that road with us.

APPENDIX A

The NPBEA 21 Domains

I. FUNCTIONAL DOMAINS

Leadership: Formulating goals with individuals or groups; initiating and maintaining direction with groups and guiding them to the accomplishment of tasks; setting priorities for one's school in the context of community and district priorities and student and staff needs; integrating own and others' ideas for task accomplishment; initiating and planning organizational change.

Information Collection: Gathering data, facts, and impressions from a variety of sources about students, parents, staff members, administrators, and community members; seeking knowledge about policies, rules, laws, precedents, or practices; managing the data flow; classifying and organizing information for use in decision making and monitoring.

Problem Analysis: Identifying the important elements of a problem situation by analyzing relevant information; framing problems; identifying possible causes; identifying additional needed information; framing and reframing possible solutions; exhibiting conceptual flexibility; assisting others to form reasoned opinions about problems and issues.

Judgment: Reaching logical conclusions and making high quality, timely decisions given the best available information.

Organizational Oversight: Planning and scheduling one's own and others' work so that resources are used appropriately, and short- and long-term priorities and goals are met; monitoring projects to meet deadlines.

Implementation: Making things happen; putting programs and plans into action; applying management technologies; applying methods of organizational change including collaborative processes; facilitating tasks; establishing progress checkpoints; considering alternative approaches; providing "midcourse" corrections when actual outcomes start to diverge from intended outcomes; adapting to new conditions.

Delegation: Assigning projects or tasks together with clear authority to accomplish them and responsibility for their timely and acceptable completion.

II. PROGRAMMATIC DOMAINS

Instructional Program: Envisioning and enabling instructional and auxiliary programs for the improvement of teaching and learning; recognizing the development needs of students; ensuring appropriate instructional methods; designing positive learning experiences; accommodating differences in cognition and achievement; mobilizing the participation of appropriate people or groups to develop these programs and to establish a positive learning environment.

Curriculum Design: Interpreting school district curricula; planning and implementing with staff a framework for instruction; initiating needs analyses and monitoring social and technological developments as they affect curriculum; responding to international content levels; adjusting content as needs and conditions change.

Student Guidance and Development: Providing for student guidance, counseling, and auxiliary services; utilizing community organizations; responding to family needs; enlisting the participation of appropriate people and groups to design and conduct these programs and to connect schooling with plans for adult life; planning for a comprehensive program of student activities.

Staff Development: Identify with participants the professional needs of individuals and groups; planning and organizing programs to improve staff effectiveness; supervising individuals and groups; engaging staff and others to plan and participate in recruitment and development; initiating self-development.

Measurement and Evaluation: Determining what diagnostic information is needed about students, staff, and the school environment; examining the extent to which outcomes meet or exceed previously defined standards, goals, or priorities for individuals or groups; drawing inferences for program revisions; interpreting measurements or evaluations for others; relating programs to desired outcomes; developing equivalent measures of competence.

Resource Allocation: Planning and developing the budget with appropriate staff; seeking, allocating, and adjusting fiscal, human, and material resources; utilizing the physical plant; monitoring resources use and reporting results.

III. INTERPERSONAL DOMAINS

Monitoring Others: Building commitment to a course of action; creating and channeling the energy of self and others; planning and encouraging participation; supporting innovation; recognizing and rewarding effective performance; providing coaching, guidance, or correction for performance that needs improvement; serving as a role model.

Sensitivity: Perceiving the needs and concerns of others; dealing with others tactfully; working with others in emotionally stressful situations or in conflict; managing conflict; obtaining feedback; recognizing multicultural sensibilities.

Oral Expression: Making oral presentations that are clear and easy to understand; clarifying and restating questions; responding, reviewing, and summarizing for groups; utilizing appropriate communicative aids; adapting for audiences.

Written Expression: Expressing ideas clearly in writing; writing appropriately for different audiences such as students, teachers, and parents; preparing brief memoranda.

IV. CONTEXTUAL DOMAINS

Philosophical and Cultural Values: Acting with a reasoned understanding of the role of education in a democratic society and in accord with accepted ethical standards; recognizing philosophical and historical influences in current social and economic issues related to education; recognizing global influences on students and society.

Legal and Regulatory Applications: Acting in accordance with regulations, laws, rules, and policies; recognizing governmental influences on education; working within local rules, procedures, and directives; administering contracts.

Policy and Political Influences: Identifying relationships between public policy and education; recognizing policy issues; examining and effecting policies individually and through professional and public groups; relating policy initiatives to the welfare of students; addressing ethical issues.

Public and Media Relationships: Developing common perceptions about school issues; interacting with parental and community opinion leaders; understanding and responding skillfully to the electronic and printed news media; initiating and reporting news through appropriate channels; enlisting public participation; recognizing and providing for market segments.

APPENDIX B

ISLLC Standards

STANDARD 1

A school administrator is an educational leader who promotes the success of all students by facilitating the development, articulation, implementation, and stewardship of a vision of learning that is shared and supported by the school community.

Knowledge

The administrator has knowledge and understanding of:

- learning goals in a pluralistic society
- the principles of developing and implementing strategic plans
- systems theory
- information sources, data collection, and data analysis strategies
- effective communication
- effective consensus-building and negotiation skills

Dispositions

The administrator believes in, values, and is committed to:

- the educability of all
- a school vision of high standards of learning
- continuous school improvement

- the inclusion of all members of the school community
- ensuring that students have the knowledge, skills, and values needed to become successful adults
- a willingness to continuously examine one's own assumptions, beliefs, and practices
- doing the work required for high levels of personal and organizational performance

Performances

The administrator facilitates, processes, and engages in activities ensuring that:

- the vision and mission of the school are effectively communicated to staff, parents, students, and community members
- the vision and mission are communicated through the use of symbols, ceremonies, stories, and similar activities
- the core beliefs of the school vision are modeled for all stakeholders
- the vision is developed with and among stakeholders
- the contributions of school community members to the realization of the vision are recognized and celebrated
- progress toward the vision and mission is communicated to all stakeholders
- the school community is involved in school improvement efforts
- the vision shapes the educational programs, plans, and actions
- an implementation plan is developed in which objectives and strategies to achieve the vision and goals are clearly articulated
- assessment data related to student learning are used to develop the school vision and goals
- relevant demographic data pertaining to students and their families are used in developing the school mission and goals
- barriers to achieving the vision are identified, clarified, and addressed
- needed resources are sought and obtained to support the implementation of the school mission and goals
- existing resources are used in support of the school vision and goals

- the vision, mission, and implementation plans are regularly monitored, evaluated, and revised

STANDARD 2

A school administrator is an educational leader who promotes the success of all students by advocating, nurturing, and sustaining a school culture and instructional program conducive to student learning and staff professional growth.

Knowledge

The administrator has knowledge and understanding of:

- student growth and development
- applied learning theories
- applied motivational theories
- curriculum design, implementation, evaluation, and refinement
- principles of effective instruction
- measurement, evaluation, and assessment strategies
- diversity and its meaning for educational programs
- adult learning and professional development models
- the change process for systems, organizations, and individuals
- the role of technology in promoting student learning and professional growth
- school cultures

Dispositions

The administrator believes in, values, and is committed to:

- student learning as the fundamental purpose of schooling
- the proposition that all students can learn
- the variety of ways in which students can learn
- lifelong learning for self and others
- professional development as an integral part of school improvement

- the benefits that diversity brings to the school community
- a safe and supportive learning environment
- preparing students to be contributing members of society

Performances

The administrator facilitates, processes, and engages in activities ensuring that:

- all individuals are treated with fairness, dignity, and respect
- professional development promotes a focus on student learning consistent with the school vision and goals
- students and staff feel valued and important
- the responsibilities and contributions of each individual are acknowledged
- barriers to student learning are identified, clarified, and addressed
- diversity is considered in developing learning experiences
- lifelong learning is encouraged and modeled
- there is a culture of high expectations for self, student, and staff performance
- technologies are used in teaching and learning
- student and staff accomplishments are recognized and celebrated
- multiple opportunities to learn are available to all students
- the school is organized and aligned for success
- curricular, cocurricular, and extracurricular programs are designed, implemented, evaluated, and refined
- curriculum decisions are based on research, expertise of teachers, and the recommendations of learned societies
- the school culture and climate are assessed on a regular basis
- a variety of sources of information is used to make decisions
- student learning is assessed using a variety of techniques
- multiple sources of information regarding performance are used by staff and students
- a variety of supervisory and evaluation models is employed
- pupil personnel programs are developed to meet the needs of students and their families

STANDARD 3

A school administrator is an educational leader who promotes the success of all students by ensuring management of the organization, operations, and resources for a safe, efficient, and effective learning environment.

Knowledge

The administrator has knowledge and understanding of:

- theories and models of organizations and the principles of organizational development
- operational procedures at the school and district level
- principles and issues relating to school safety and security
- human resources management and development
- principles and issues relating to fiscal operations of school management
- principles and issues relating to school facilities and use of space
- legal issues impacting school operations
- current technologies that support management functions

Dispositions

The administrator believes in, values, and is committed to:

- making management decisions to enhance learning and teaching
- taking risks to improve schools
- trusting people and their judgments
- accepting responsibility
- high-quality standards, expectations, and performances
- involving stakeholders in management processes
- a safe environment

Performances

The administrator facilitates, processes, and engages in activities ensuring that:

- knowledge of learning, teaching, and student development is used to inform management decisions

- operational procedures are designed and managed to maximize opportunities for successful learning
- emerging trends are recognized, studied, and applied as appropriate
- operational plans and procedures to achieve the vision and goals of the school are in place
- collective bargaining and other contractual agreements related to the school are effectively managed
- the school plant, equipment, and support systems operate safely, efficiently, and effectively
- time is managed to maximize attainment of organizational goals
- potential problems and opportunities are identified
- problems are confronted and resolved in a timely manner
- financial, human, and material resources are aligned to the goals of schools
- the school acts entrepreneurally to support continuous improvement
- organizational systems are regularly monitored and modified as needed
- stakeholders are involved in decisions affecting schools
- responsibility is shared to maximize ownership and accountability
- effective problem-framing and problem-solving skills are used
- effective conflict-resolution skills are used
- effective group-process and consensus-building skills are used
- effective communication skills are used
- a safe, clean, and aesthetically pleasing school environment is created and maintained
- human resource functions support the attainment of school goals
- confidentiality and privacy of school records are maintained

STANDARD 4

A school administrator is an educational leader who promotes the success of all students by collaborating with families and community members, responding to diverse community interests and needs, and mobilizing community resources.

Knowledge

The administrator has knowledge and understanding of:

- emerging issues and trends that potentially impact the school community
- the conditions and dynamics of the diverse school community
- community resources
- community relations and marketing strategies and processes
- successful models of school, family, business, community, government, and higher education partnerships

Dispositions

The administrator believes in, values, and is committed to:

- schools operating as an integral part of the larger community
- collaboration and communication with families
- involvement of families and other stakeholders in school decision-making processes
- the proposition that diversity enriches the school
- families as partners in the education of their children
- the proposition that families have the best interests of their children in mind
- resources of the family and community needing to be brought to bear on the education of students
- an informed public

Performances

The administrator facilitates, processes, and engages in activities ensuring that:

- high visibility, active involvement, and communication with the larger community is a priority
- relationships with community leaders are identified and nurtured
- information about family and community concerns, expectations, and needs is used regularly

- there is outreach to different business, religious, political, and service agencies and organizations
- credence is given to individuals and groups whose values and opinions may conflict
- the school and community serve one another as resources
- available community resources are secured to help the school solve problems and achieve goals
- partnerships are established with area businesses, institutions of higher education, and community groups to strengthen programs and support school goals
- community youth family services are integrated with school programs
- community stakeholders are treated equitably
- diversity is recognized and valued
- effective media relations are developed and maintained
- a comprehensive program of community relations is established
- public resources and funds are used appropriately and wisely
- community collaboration is modeled for staff
- opportunities for staff to develop collaborative skills are provided

STANDARD 5

A school administrator is an educational leader who promotes the success of all students by acting with integrity, fairness, and in an ethical manner.

Knowledge

The administrator has knowledge and understanding of:

- the purpose of education and the role of leadership in modern society
- various ethical frameworks and perspectives on ethics
- the values of the diverse school community
- professional codes of ethics
- the philosophy and history of education

Dispositions

The administrator believes in, values, and is committed to:

- the ideal of the common good
- the principles in the Bill of Rights
- the right of every student to a free, quality education
- bringing ethical principles to the decision-making process
- subordinating one's own interest to the good of the school community
- accepting the consequences for upholding one's principles and actions
- using the influence of one's office constructively and productively in the service of all students and their families
- development of a caring school community

Performances

The administrator:

- examines personal and professional values
- demonstrates a personal and professional code of ethics
- demonstrates values, beliefs, and attitudes that inspire others to higher levels of performance
- serves as a role model
- accepts responsibility for school operations
- considers the impact of one's administrative practices on others
- uses the influence of the office to enhance the educational program rather than for personal gain
- treats people fairly, equitably, and with dignity and respect
- protects the rights and confidentiality of students and staff
- demonstrates appreciation for and sensitivity to the diversity in the school community
- recognizes and respects the legitimate authority of others
- examines and considers the prevailing values of the diverse school community
- expects that others in the school community will demonstrate integrity and exercise ethical behavior

- opens the school to public scrutiny
- fulfills legal and contractual obligations
- applies laws and procedures fairly, wisely, and considerately

STANDARD 6

A school administrator is an educational leader who promotes the success of all students by understanding, responding to, and influencing the larger political, social, economic, legal, and cultural context.

Knowledge

The administrator has knowledge and understanding of:

- principles of representative governance that undergird the system of American schools
- the role of public education in developing and renewing a democratic society and an economically productive nation
- the law as related to education and schooling
- the political, social, cultural, and economic systems and processes that impact schools
- models and strategies of change and conflict resolution as applied to the larger political, social, cultural, and economic contexts of schooling
- global issues and forces affecting teaching and learning
- the dynamics of policy development and advocacy under our democratic political system
- the importance of diversity and equity in a democratic society

Dispositions

The administrator believes in, values, and is committed to:

- education as a key to opportunity and social mobility
- recognizing a variety of ideas, values, and cultures
- importance of a continuing dialogue with other decision makers affecting education

- actively participating in the political and policy-making context in the service of education
- using legal systems to protect student rights and improve student opportunities

Performances

The administrator facilitates, processes, and engages in activities ensuring that:

- the environment in which schools operate is influenced on behalf of students and their families
- communication occurs among the school community concerning trends, issues, and potential changes in the environment in which schools operate
- there is ongoing dialogue with representatives of diverse community groups
- the school community works within the framework of policies, laws, and regulations enacted by local, state, and federal authorities
- public policy is shaped to provide quality education for students

APPENDIX C

Interstate New Teacher Assessment and Support Consortium (INTASC) Standards

STANDARD 1: SUBJECT MATTER

The teacher understands the central concepts, tools of inquiry, and structures of the discipline(s) he or she teaches and can create learning experiences that make these aspects of subject matter meaningful for students.

Knowledge

- The teacher understands major concepts, assumptions, debates, processes of inquiry, and ways of knowing that are central to the discipline(s) s/he teaches.
- The teacher understands how students' conceptual frameworks and their misconceptions for an area of knowledge can influence their learning.
- The teacher can relate his/her disciplinary knowledge to other subject areas.

Dispositions

- The teacher realizes that subject matter knowledge is not a fixed body of facts but is complex and ever-evolving. S/he seeks to keep abreast of new ideas and understandings in the field.
- The teacher appreciates multiple perspectives and conveys to learners how knowledge is developed from the vantage point of the knower.

- The teacher has enthusiasm for the discipline(s) s/he teaches and sees connections to everyday life.
- The teacher is committed to continuous learning and engages in professional discourse about subject matter knowledge and children's learning of the discipline.

Performances

- The teacher effectively uses multiple representations and explanations of disciplinary concepts that capture key ideas and link them to students' prior understandings.
- The teacher can represent and use differing viewpoints, theories, "ways of knowing," and methods of inquiry in his/her teaching of subject matter concepts.
- The teacher can evaluate teaching resources and curriculum materials for their comprehensiveness, accuracy, and usefulness for representing particular ideas and concepts.
- The teacher engages students in generating knowledge and testing hypotheses according to the methods of inquiry and standards of evidence used in the discipline.
- The teacher develops and uses curricula that encourage students to see, question, and interpret ideas from diverse perspectives.
- The teacher can create interdisciplinary learning experiences that allow students to integrate knowledge, skills, and methods of inquiry from several subject areas.

STANDARD 2: STUDENT LEARNING

The teacher understands how children and youth learn and develop, and can provide learning opportunities that support their intellectual, social, and personal development.

Knowledge

- The teacher understands how learning occurs—how students construct knowledge, acquire skills, and develop habits of mind—and knows how to use instructional strategies that promote student learning.

- The teacher understands that students' physical, social, emotional, moral, and cognitive development influence learning and knows how to address these factors when making instructional decisions.
- The teacher is aware of expected developmental progressions and ranges of individual variation within each domain (physical, social, emotional, moral, and cognitive), can identify levels of readiness in learning, and understands how development in any one domain may affect performance in others.

Dispositions

- The teacher appreciates individual variation within each area of development, shows respect for the diverse talents of all learners, and is committed to help them develop self-confidence and competence.
- The teacher is disposed to use students' strengths as a basis for growth, and their errors as an opportunity for learning.

Performances

- The teacher assesses individual and group performance in order to design instruction that meets learners' current needs in each domain (cognitive, social, emotional, moral, and physical), and that leads to the next level of development.
- The teacher stimulates student reflection on prior knowledge and links new ideas to already familiar ideas, making connections to students' experiences, providing opportunities for active engagement, manipulation, and testing of ideas and materials, and encouraging students to assume responsibility for shaping their learning tasks.
- The teacher accesses students' thinking and experiences as a basis for instructional activities by, for example, encouraging discussion, listening and responding to group interaction, and eliciting samples of student thinking orally and in writing.

STANDARD 3: DIVERSE LEARNERS

The teacher understands how students differ in their approaches to learning and creates instructional opportunities that are adapted to learners from diverse cultural backgrounds and with exceptionalities.

Knowledge

- The teacher understands and can identify differences in approaches to learning and performance, including different learning styles, multiple intelligences, and performance modes, and can design instruction that helps use students' strengths as the basis for growth.
- The teacher knows about areas of exceptionality in learning, including learning disabilities, visual and perceptual difficulties, special physical or mental challenges, and gifted and talented.
- The teacher knows about the process of second language acquisition and about strategies to support the learning of students whose first language is not English.
- The teacher understands how students' learning is influenced by individual experiences, talents, and prior learning, as well as language, culture, family, and community values.
- The teacher has a well-grounded framework for understanding cultural and community diversity and knows how to learn about and incorporate students' experiences, cultures, and community resources into instruction.

Dispositions

- The teacher believes that all children can learn at high levels and persists in helping all children achieve success.
- The teacher appreciates and values human diversity, shows respect for students' varied talents and perspectives, and is committed to the pursuit of "individually configured excellence."
- The teacher respects students as individuals with differing personal and family backgrounds and various skills, talents, and interest.
- The teacher is sensitive to community and cultural norms.
- The teacher makes students feel valued for their potential as people, and helps them learn to value each other.

Performances

- The teacher identifies and designs instruction appropriate to students' stages of development, learning styles, strengths, and needs.
- The teacher uses teaching approaches that are sensitive to the multiple experiences of learners and that address different learning and performance modes.
- The teacher makes appropriate provision (in terms of time and circumstances for work, tasks assigned, communication and response modes) for individual students who have particular learning differences or needs.
- The teacher can identify when and how to access appropriate services or resources to meet exceptional learning needs.
- The teacher seeks to understand students' families, cultures, and communities, and uses this information as a basis for connecting instruction to students' experiences (e.g., drawing explicit connections between subject matter and community matters, making assignments that can be related to students' experiences and cultures).
- The teacher brings multiple perspectives to the discussion of subject matter, including attention to students' personal, family, and community experiences and cultural norms.
- The teacher creates a learning community in which individual differences are respected.

STANDARD 4: INSTRUCTIONAL STRATEGIES

The teacher understands and uses a variety of instructional strategies to encourage students' development of critical thinking, problem solving, and performance skills.

Knowledge

- The teacher understands the cognitive processes associated with various kinds of learning (e.g., critical and creative thinking, problem structuring and problem solving, invention, memorization and recall) and how these processes can be stimulated.
- The teacher understands the principles and techniques, along with advantages and limitations, associated with various instructional

strategies (e.g., cooperative learning, direct instruction, discovery learning, whole group discussion, independent study, interdisciplinary instruction).

- The teacher knows how to enhance learning through the use of a wide variety of materials as well as human and technological resources (e.g., computers, audio-visual technologies, videotapes and discs, local experts, primary documents and artifacts, texts, reference books, literature, and other print resources).

Dispositions

- The teacher values the development of students' critical thinking, independent problem solving, and performance capabilities.
- The teacher values flexibility and reciprocity in the teaching process as necessary for adapting instruction to student responses, ideas, and needs.
- The teacher values the use of educational technology in the teaching and learning process.

Performances

- The teacher carefully evaluates how to achieve learning goals, choosing alternative teaching strategies and materials to achieve different instructional purposes and to meet student needs (e.g., developmental stages, prior knowledge, learning styles, and interests).
- The teacher uses multiple teaching and learning strategies to engage students in active learning opportunities that promote the development of critical thinking, problem solving, and performance capabilities that help students assume responsibility for identifying and using learning resources.
- The teacher constantly monitors and adjusts strategies in response to learner feedback.
- The teacher varies his or her role in the instructional process (e.g., instructor, facilitator, coach, and audience) in relation to the content and purposes of instruction and the needs of students.
- The teacher develops a variety of clear, accurate presentations and representations of concepts, using alternative explanations to assist

students' understanding, and presenting diverse perspective to encourage critical thinking.
- The teacher uses educational technology to broaden student knowledge about technology, to deliver instruction to students at different levels and paces, and for advanced levels of learning.

STANDARD 5: LEARNING ENVIRONMENT

The teacher uses an understanding of individual and group motivation and behavior to create a learning environment that encourages positive social interaction, active engagement in learning, and self-motivation.

Knowledge

- The teacher can use knowledge about human motivation and behavior drawn from the foundational sciences of psychology, anthropology, and sociology to develop strategies for organizing and supporting individual and group work.
- The teacher understands how social groups function and influence people, and how people influence groups.
- The teacher knows how to help people work productively and cooperatively with each other in complex social settings.
- The teacher understands the principles of effective classroom management and can use a range of strategies to promote positive relationships, cooperation, and purposeful learning in the classroom.
- The teacher recognizes factors and situations that are likely to promote or diminish intrinsic motivation, and knows how to help students become self-motivated.

Dispositions

- The teacher takes responsibility for establishing a positive climate in the classroom and participates in maintaining such a climate in the school as a whole.
- The teacher understands how participation supports commitment, and is committed to the expression and use of democratic values in the classroom.

- The teacher values the role of students in promoting each other's learning and recognizes the importance of peer relationships in establishing a climate of learning.
- The teacher recognizes the values of intrinsic motivation to students' lifelong growth and learning.
- The teacher is committed to the continuous development of individual students' abilities and considers how different motivational strategies are likely to encourage this development for each student.

Performances

- The teacher creates a smoothly functioning learning community in which students assume responsibility for themselves and one another, participate in decision making, work collaboratively and independently, and engage in purposeful learning activities.
- The teacher engages students in individual and group learning activities that help them develop the motivation to achieve, by, for example, relating lessons to students' personal interests, allowing students to have choices in their learning, and leading students to ask questions and pursue problems that are meaningful to them.
- The teacher organizes, allocates, and manages the resources of time, space, activities, and attention to provide active and equitable engagement of students in productive tasks.
- The teacher maximizes the amount of class time spent in learning by creating expectations and processes for communication and behavior along with a physical setting conducive to classroom goals.
- The teacher helps the group to develop shared values and expectations for student interactions, academic discussions, and individual and group responsibility that create a positive classroom climate of openness, mutual respect, support, and inquiry.
- The teacher analyzes the classroom environment and makes decisions and adjustments to enhance social relationships, student motivation and engagement, and productive work.
- The teacher organizes, prepares students for, and monitors independent and group work that allows for full and varied participation of all individuals.

STANDARD 6: COMMUNICATION

The teacher uses knowledge of effective verbal, nonverbal, and media communication techniques to foster active inquiry, collaboration, and supportive interaction in the classroom.

Knowledge

- The teacher understands communication theory, language development, and the role of language in learning.
- The teacher understands how cultural and gender differences can affect communication in the classroom.
- The teacher recognizes the importance of nonverbal as well as verbal communication.
- The teacher knows about and can use effective verbal, nonverbal, and media communication techniques.

Dispositions

- The teacher recognizes the power of language for fostering self-expression, identity development, and learning.
- The teacher values many ways in which people seek to communicate and encourages many modes of communication in the classroom.
- The teacher is a thoughtful and responsive listener.
- The teacher appreciates the cultural dimensions of communication, responds appropriately, and seeks to foster culturally sensitive communication by and among all students in the class.

Performances

- The teacher models effective communications strategies in conveying ideas and information and in asking questions (e.g., monitoring the effects of messages; restating ideas and drawing connections; using visual, aural, and kinesthetic cues; and being sensitive to nonverbal cues given and received).
- The teacher supports and expands learner expression in speaking, writing, and other media.

- The teacher knows how to ask questions and stimulate discussion in different ways for particular purposes, for example, probing for learner understanding, and helping students articulate their ideas and thinking processes, promoting risk-taking and problem-solving, facilitating factual recall, encouraging convergent and divergent thinking, stimulating curiosity, and helping stimulate students to question.
- The teacher communicates in ways that demonstrate a sensitivity to cultural and gender differences (e.g., appropriate use of eye contact, interpretation of body language and verbal statements, acknowledgment of and responsiveness to different modes of communication and participation).
- The teacher knows how to use a variety of media communication tools, including audio-visual aids and computers, including educational technology, to enrich learning opportunities.

STANDARD 7: PLANNING INSTRUCTION

The teacher plans and manages instruction based upon knowledge of subject matter, students, the community, and curriculum goals.

Knowledge

- The teacher understands learning theory, subject matter, curriculum development, and student development and knows how to use this knowledge in planning instruction to meet curriculum goals.
- The teacher knows how to take contextual considerations (instructional materials, individual student interests, needs, and aptitudes, and community resources) into account in planning instruction that creates an effective bridge between curriculum goals and students' experiences.
- The teacher knows when and how to adjust plans based on student responses and other contingencies.

Dispositions

- The teacher values both long-term and short-term planning.
- The teacher believes that plans must always be open to adjustment and revision based on student needs and changing circumstances.
- The teacher values planning as a collegial activity.

Performances

- As an individual and a member of a team, the teacher selects and creates learning experiences that are appropriate for curriculum goals, relevant to learners, and based upon principles of effective instruction (e.g., that activate students' prior knowledge, anticipate preconceptions, encourage exploration and problem solving, and build new skills on those previously acquired).
- The teacher plans for learning opportunities that recognize and address variation in learning styles and performance modes.
- The teacher creates lessons and activities that operate at multiple levels to meet the developmental and individual needs of diverse learners and help each progress.
- The teacher creates short-range and long-term plans that are linked to student needs and performance, and adapts the plans to ensure and capitalize on student progress and motivation.
- The teacher responds to unanticipated sources of input, evaluates plans in relation to short- and long-range goals, and systematically adjusts plans to meet student needs and enhance learning.

STANDARD 8: ASSESSMENT

The teacher understands and uses formal and informal assessment strategies to evaluate and ensure the continuous intellectual, social, and physical development of the learner.

Knowledge

- The teacher understands the characteristics, uses, advantages, and limitations of different types of assessments (e.g., criterion-referenced and norm-referenced instruments, traditional standardized and performance-based tests, observation systems, and assessments of student work) for evaluating how students learn, what they know and are able to do, and what kinds of experiences and technology will support their further growth and development.
- The teacher knows how to select, construct, and use assessment strategies, technology, and instruments appropriate to the learning outcomes being evaluated and to other diagnostic purposes.

- The teacher understands measurement theory and assessment-related issues, such as validity, reliability, bias, and scoring concerns.

Dispositions

- The teacher values ongoing assessment as essential to the instructional process and recognizes that many different assessment strategies, accurately and systematically used, are necessary for monitoring and promoting student learning.
- The teacher is committed to using assessment to identify student strengths and promote student growth rather than to deny students access to learning opportunities.

Performances

- The teacher appropriately uses a variety of formal and informal assessment techniques (e.g., observation, portfolios of student work, teacher-made tests, performance tasks, projects, student self-assessments, peer assessment, and standardized tests) to enhance her or his knowledge of learners, evaluate students' progress and performances, and modify teaching and learning strategies.
- The teacher solicits and uses information about students' experiences, learning behavior, needs, and progress from parents, other colleagues, and the students themselves.
- The teacher uses assessment strategies to involve learners in self-assessment activities, to help them become aware of their strengths and needs, and to encourage them to set personal goals for learning.
- The teacher evaluates the effect of class activities on both individuals and the class as a whole, collecting information through observation of classroom interactions, questioning, and analysis of student work.
- The teacher monitors her/his own teaching strategies and behavior in relation to student success, modifying plans and instructional approaches accordingly.
- The teacher maintains useful records of student work and performance and can communicate student progress knowledgeably

and responsibly, based on appropriate indicators, to students, parents/guardians, and other colleagues.

STANDARD 9: REFLECTION AND PROFESSIONAL DEVELOPMENT

The teacher is a reflective practitioner who continually evaluates the effects of her/his choices and actions on others (students, parents, and other professionals in the learning community) and who actively seeks out opportunities to grow professionally.

Knowledge

- The teacher understands the historical and philosophical foundations of education.
- The teacher understands methods of inquiry that provide him/her with a variety of self-assessment and problem-solving strategies for reflecting on his/her practice, its influences on students' growth and learning, and the complex interactions between them.
- The teacher is aware of major areas of research on teaching and of resources available for professional learning (e.g., professional literature, colleagues, professional associations, professional development activities).

Dispositions

- The teacher values critical thinking and self-directed learning as habits of mind.
- The teacher is committed to reflection, assessment, and learning as an ongoing process.
- The teacher is willing to give and receive help.
- The teacher is committed to seeking out, developing, and continually refining practices that address the individual needs of students.
- The teacher recognizes her/his professional responsibility for engaging in and supporting appropriate professional practices for self and colleagues.

Performances

- The teacher uses classroom observation, information about students, and research as sources for evaluating the outcomes of teaching and learning and as a basis for experimenting with, reflecting on, and revising practice.
- The teacher seeks out professional literature, colleagues, and other resources to support her/his own development as a learner and a teacher.
- The teacher draws upon professional colleagues within the school and other professional arenas as supports for reflection, problem-solving and new ideas, actively sharing experiences and seeking and giving feedback.

STANDARD 10: COLLABORATION, ETHICS, AND RELATIONSHIPS

The teacher communicates and interacts with parents/guardians, families, school colleagues, and the community to support students' learning and well-being.

Knowledge

- The teacher understands schools as organizations within the larger community context and understands the operations of the relevant aspects of the system(s) within s/he works.
- The teacher understands how factors in the students' environment outside of school (e.g., family circumstances, community environments, health and economic conditions) may influence students' life and learning.
- The teacher understands and implements laws related to students' rights and teacher responsibilities (e.g., for equal education, appropriate education for students with disabilities, confidentiality, privacy, appropriate treatment of students, and reporting in situations related to possible child abuse).

Dispositions

- The teacher values and appreciates the importance of all aspects of a child's experience.

- The teacher is concerned about all aspects of a child's well-being (cognitive, emotional, social, and physical), and is alert to signs of difficulties.
- The teacher respects the privacy of students and confidentiality of information.
- The teacher is willing to consult with other adults regarding the education and well-being of her/his students.
- The teacher is willing to work with other professionals to improve the overall learning environment for students.

Performances

- The teacher participates in collegial activities designed to make the entire school a productive learning environment.
- The teacher makes links with the learners' other environments on behalf of students, by consulting with parents, counselors, teachers of other classes and activities within the schools, and professionals in other community agencies.
- The teacher can identify and use community resources to foster student learning.
- The teacher establishes respectful and productive relationships with parents and guardians from diverse home and community situations, and seeks to develop cooperative partnerships in support of student learning and well being.
- The teacher talks with and listens to the student, is sensitive and responsive to clues of distress, investigates situations, and seeks outside help as needed and appropriate to remedy problems.
- The teacher acts as an advocate for students.

APPENDIX D

The Five Propositions of Accomplished Teaching

The National Board for Professional Teaching Standards seeks to identify and recognize teachers who effectively enhance student learning and demonstrate the high level of knowledge, skills, abilities, and commitments reflected in the following five core propositions.

1. Teachers are committed to students and their learning.

    - Accomplished teachers are dedicated to making knowledge accessible to all students. They act on the belief that all students can learn. They treat students equitably, recognizing the individual differences that distinguish one student from another and taking account of these differences in their practice. They adjust their practice based on observation and knowledge of their students' interests, abilities, skills, knowledge, family circumstances, and peer relationships.
    - Accomplished teachers understand how students develop and learn. They incorporate the prevailing theories of cognition and intelligence in their practice. They are aware of the influence of context and culture on behavior. They develop students' cognitive capacity and their respect for learning. Equally important, they foster students' self-esteem, motivation, character, civic responsibility, and their respect for individual, cultural, religious, and racial differences.

2. Teachers know the subjects they teach and how to teach those subjects.

    - Accomplished teachers have a rich understanding of the subject(s) they teach and appreciate how knowledge in their subject is created, organized, linked to other disciplines, and applied to real-world settings. While faithfully representing the collective wisdom of our culture and upholding the value of disciplinary knowledge, they also develop the critical and analytical capacities of their students.
    - Accomplished teachers command specialized knowledge of how to convey and reveal subject matter to students. They are aware of the preconceptions and background knowledge that students typically bring to each subject and of strategies and instructional materials that can be of assistance. They understand where difficulties are likely to arise and modify their practice accordingly. Their instructional repertoire allows them to create multiple paths to the subjects they teach, and they are adept at teaching students how to pose and solve their own problems.

3. Teachers are responsible for managing and monitoring student learning.

    - Accomplished teachers create, enrich, maintain, and alter instructional settings to capture and sustain the interest of their students and to make the most effective use of time. They also are adept at engaging students and adults to assist their teaching and at enlisting their colleagues' knowledge and expertise to complement their own.
    - Accomplished teachers command a range of generic instructional techniques, know when each is appropriate, and can implement them as needed. They are as aware of ineffectual or damaging practice as they are devoted to elegant practice. They know how to engage groups of students to ensure a disciplined learning environment, and how to organize instruction to allow the schools' goals for students to be met. They are adept at setting norms for social interaction among students and between students and teachers. They understand how to motivate stu-

dents to learn and how to maintain their interest even in the face of temporary failure.

- Accomplished teachers can assess the progress of individual students as well as that of the class as a whole. They employ multiple methods for measuring student growth and understanding and can clearly explain student performance to parents.

4. Teachers think systematically about their practice and learn from experience.

   - Accomplished teachers are models of educated persons, exemplifying the virtues they seek to inspire in students—curiosity, tolerance, honesty, fairness, respect for diversity and appreciation of cultural differences—and the capacities that are prerequisites for intellectual growth: the ability to reason and take multiple perspectives to be creative and take risks, and to adopt an experimental and problem-solving orientation.
   - Accomplished teachers draw on their knowledge of human development, subject matter and instruction, and their understanding of their students to make principled judgments about sound practice. Their decisions are not only grounded in the literature but also in their experience. They engage in lifelong learning, which they seek to encourage in their students.
   - Striving to strengthen their teaching, accomplished teachers critically examine their practice, seek to expand their repertoire, deepen their knowledge, sharpen their judgment, and adapt their teaching to new findings, ideas, and theories.

5. Teachers are members of learning communities.

   - Accomplished teachers contribute to the effectiveness of the school by working collaboratively with other professionals on instructional policy, curriculum development, and staff development. They can evaluate school progress and the allocation of school resources in light of their understanding of state and local educational objectives. They are knowledgeable about specialized school and community resources that can be engaged for their students' benefit, and are skilled at employing such resources as needed.

- Accomplished teachers find ways to work collaboratively and creatively with parents, engaging them productively in the work of the school.

References

Barnet, B., F. McQuarrie, and J. Norris, eds. 1991. *The moral imperatives of leadership.* Memphis, Tenn.: National Policy Board for Educational Administration.

Baron, R. 1996. Interpersonal relations in organizations. In *Individual differences and behavior in organizations,* ed. K. Murphy, 334–70. San Francisco: Jossey-Bass.

Blake, R., and J. Mouton. 1964. *The managerial grid.* Houston, Tex.: Gulf Publishing.

Bridges, W. 1991. *Managing transitions: Making the most of change.* Reading, Mass.: Addison-Wesley.

Caine, D. 1999. *Within reason.* New York: Pantheon.

Chaiken, S., D. Gruenfeld, and C. Judd. 2000. Persuasion in negotiations and conflict situations. In *The handbook of conflict resolution: Theory and practice,* eds. M. Deutsch and P. Coleman, 144–65. San Francisco: Jossey-Bass.

Cherniss, C. 2000. Social and emotional competence in the workplace. In *The handbook of emotional intelligence: Theory, development, assessment, and application at home, school and in the workplace*, eds. R. Bar-On and J. Parker. San Francisco: Jossey-Bass.

Christians, C., K. Rotzoll, and M. Fackler. 1983. *Media ethics: Cases and moral reasoning*. Philadelphia: Annenberg/Longman Communication.

Confucius. [1938] 2000. *The analects*. Trans. A Walzy. New York: Vintage.

Cooper, R., and A. Sawaf. 1997. *Executive EQ: Emotional intelligence in leadership and organizations*. New York: Grosset/Putnam.

Dommoyer, R., M. Imber, and J. Scheurich, eds. 1995. *The knowledge base in educational administration*. New York: SUNY Press.

Ehninger, D. 1972. *Contemporary rhetoric*. Glenview, Ill.: Scott Foresman.

Foster, W. 1989. Toward a critical practice of leadership. In *Critical perspectives on educational leadership*, ed. J. Smyth, 39–62. New York: Falmer.

Gardner, H. 1995. *Leading minds*. New York: Basic.

Goleman, D. 1995. *Emotional intelligence*. New York: Bantam.

Goodnough, A. 2001. For Levy, can-do business style runs into education reality. *New York Times,* 9 April.

Greenstein, F. I. 2000. *The presidential difference: Leadership styles from FDR to Clinton.* New York: Martin Kessler Books.

Hackman, J., ed. 1990. *Groups that work (and those that don't).* San Francisco: Jossey-Bass.

Hayles, R., and A. Mendez-Russell. 1997. *The diversity initiative: Why some fail and what to do about it.* Chicago: American Society for Training and Development.

Hegal, G. [1837] 1953. *Reason in history.* Trans. R. Hartman. Indianapolis, Ind.: Bobbs Merrill.

Hollenbeck, J., J. Lepine, and D. Ilgen. 1996. Adapting to roles in decision-making teams. In *Individual differences and behavior in organizations,* ed. K. Murphy, 300–33. San Francisco: Jossey-Bass.

Husserl, E. [1785] 1962. *Ideas: General introduction to pure phenomenology.* Trans. W. Gibson. New York: Collier.

Jossey-Bass Reader on Educational Leadership, The. 2000. San Francisco: Jossey-Bass.

Kant, I. [1785] 1964. *Groundwork of the metaphysics of morals*. Trans. H. Paton. New York: Harper & Row.

Kelley, C. 1999. Leveraging human and fiscal resources for school improvement. *Educational Administration Quarterly* 35(4): 642–57.

Kouzes, J.M. and Posner, B.Z. 1993. Credibility: How Leaders Gain and Lose It, Why People Demand It.

Krauss, R., and E. Morsella. 2000. Communication and conflict. In *The handbook of conflict resolution: Theory and practice,* eds. M. Deutsch and P. Coleman, 131–43. San Francisco: Jossey-Bass.

Lavine, T. 1984. *From Socrates to Sartre: The philosophic quest.* New York: Bantam.

Machiavelli, N. [1527] 1952. *The Prince.* New York: New American Library.

Maxcy, S. 1991. *Educational leadership: A critical pragmatic perspective.* New York: Bergin & Garvey.

McCall, M., M. Lombardo, and A. Morrison. 1988. *The lessons of experience: How successful executives develop on the job.* New York: Lexington.

McCauley, C., R. Moxley, and E. Velsor, eds. 1998. *The Center of Creative Leadership handbook of leadership development.* San Francisco: Jossey-Bass.

Michaels, V. 2000. Do first, talk later, trumps Blake. *USA Today,* 26 October.

Morgan, G. 1997. *Images of civilization.* 3rd ed. Thousand Oaks, Calif.: Sage.

Mysteries of the genes. 2001. *The New York Times,* 17 February.

Northouse, P. 2001. *Leadership: Theory and practice*. Thousand Oaks, Calif.: Sage.

Olson, S. 2001. The genetic archaeology of race. *The Atlantic* 287(4): 69–80.

Plato. 1974. *The republic.* Trans. G. Garube. Indianapolis, Ind.: Hackett.

Purpel, D. 1989. *The moral and spiritual crisis in education.* New York: Bergin & Gravey.

Rawls, J. 1971. *A theory of justice.* Cambridge, Mass.: Harvard University Press.

Salovey, P., and J. Mayer. 1990. *Emotional intelligence: Imagination, cognition, and personality*. 9, 185–211.

Senge, P. 1999. The practice of innovation. In *Leader to leader*, ed. F. Hesselbein and P. Cohen, 57–68. San Francisco: Jossey-Bass.

Sergiovanni, T. 1992. *Moral leadership: Getting to the heart of school improvement.* San Francisco: Jossey-Bass.

Starratt, R. 1991. Building an ethical school: A theory for practice in educational leadership. *Educational Administration Quarterly* 27(2): 185–202.

Strike, K., E. Haller, and J. Soltis. 1998. *The ethics of school administration.* 2nd ed. New York: Teachers College.

Tinker, C. 1989. Can we be good without God? *The Atlantic Monthly* (December): 69–85.

Wilson, E. 1998. *Consilience*. New York: Albert A. Knopf.

Wilson, J. 1994. *The moral sense*. New York: Free Press.

Further Readings

NEUROCOGNITIVE RESEARCH

Caine, D. *Within Reason.* (New York: Pantheon Books, 1999).

Caine is a Canadian neurologist who combines hard scientific evidence with informed speculation to describe the role of the emotions in cognitive thought and decision making. He contends, "Reason lacks the capacity to motivate because it cannot make us feel anything. Its nature does not include any direct link to mental rewards, although it is, of course, always available to be applied to a task that entails a reward" (27). Caine is a strong proponent of the notion that emotion drives reason.

Carter, R. *Mapping the Mind.* (Berkeley: University of California Press, 1998).

Carter is a professional writer who provides a lucid explanation of the brain-imaging techniques such as Functional Magnetic Resonance Imaging (fMRI) that are being used to explore the brain. This technology has been instrumental in graphically illustrating how the emotions affect behavior.

Damasio, A. *Descartes' Error: Emotion, Reason, and the Human Brain.* (New York: Avon Books, 1994).

Descartes's error was his belief in the separation of the mind and the body. Damasio is a neurologist who uses the evidence of surgical procedure to illustrate Descartes's mistake. Damasio has compiled the largest file of surgical cases in existence that specifically shows how the emotions and behavior are affected by trauma to the brain.

LeDoux, J. *The Emotional Brain.* (New York: Touchstone, 1996).

LeDoux is a neurologist studying neural networks associated with the emotions. LeDoux points out that accepting new research about the emotions will change not only the way we think about the emotions but also the way we think about the nature of humans.

Pert, C. *Molecules of Emotion.* (New York: Scribner, 1997).

Pert is a biologist who interweaves fascinating research at the molecular level with stories of her adventures as a scientist at the National Institutes of Health. Molecular research supports the assertion that the emotions streamline and inform decision making.

Pinker, S. *How the Mind Works.* (New York: Norton, 1997).

Pinker is a linguist whose main focus is not the emotions. His aim is to provide a comprehensive explanation of how the mind works. His description of the complex workings of the brain supports the idea of the importance of the emotions in rational thought.

Sylwester, R. *A Celebration of Neurons: An Educator's Guide to the Human Brain.* (Alexandria, Va.: ASCD, 1995).

Sylwester is an educator who applies recent neurological research to learning and teaching. He describes a model of human behavior in which the emotions drive attention, attention drives memory, and memory drives learning.

LEADERSHIP FAILURE

Bulach, C., D. Boothe, and W. Pickett. "'Should nots' for school principals: Teachers share their views." *ERS Spectrum: Journal of School Research and Information* 10 (1998): 16–20.

This study features a statistical analysis of the perceived negative behaviors reported by subordinates about their school leaders. The most often reported negative leadership behaviors were in the areas of human relations and communication.

Davis, S. "Superintendents' perspectives on the involuntary departure of public school principals: The most frequent reason why principals lose their jobs." *Education Administrative Quarterly* 34 (1998): 58–90.

Davis conducted a statistical analysis of superintendents' perceptions of why principals fail. Human relations constituted the most commonly cited reason that principals lost their jobs.

Leslie, J., and E. Van Velsor. *A Look at Derailment Today: Europe and the United States.* (Greensboro, N.C.: Center for Creative Leadership, 1996).

Leslie and Van Velsor are consultants at the Center for Creative Leadership. They found that one of the primary reasons top American and European executives failed in their positions was a failure to build or lead a team.

NETWORKING

House, R. "Path-goal theory of leadership: Lessons, legacy, and a reformulated theory." *Leadership Quarterly* 7 (1996): 323–52.

House, the author of the path-goal leadership theory, has reformulated the theory and added four additional leadership behaviors. One of the additional leadership behaviors he calls group-work representation and networking. Each of the behaviors House describes is essential to effective leadership.

Morrison, A. *The New Leader: Guidelines on Leadership Destiny in America.* (San Francisco: Jossey-Bass, 1992).

In a section on the advantages of networking, Morrison shows how networking enhances the leader's organizational savvy. He also details the value of informal organizational information grapevines.

EMOTIONAL INTELLIGENCE

Bar-On, R., and J. Parker, eds. *The Handbook of Emotional Intelligence: Theory, Development, Assessment, and Application at Home, School, and in the Workplace.* (Jossey-Bass: San Francisco, 2000).

This book provides the most comprehensive and thorough exploration of the concept of emotional intelligence available.

Goleman, D. *Emotional Intelligence.* (New York: Bantam, 1995).

This is the best-selling book that brought the concept of emotional intelligence to the attention of the general public. Goleman describes the concept in clear, understandable language and uses lively anecdotes and cases to illustrate the importance of emotional intelligence in decision making and behavior.

Goleman, D. *Working with Emotional Intelligence.* (New York: Bantam, 1998).

A follow-up to his original work, Goleman tells how emotional intelligence can be applied to various aspects of leadership and communication. Goleman states that an analysis of leadership competency models from all over the world indicates that emotional competencies rather than technical competencies make up 80 to 100 percent of the skills listed by organizations as essential for success in leadership.

TEAMING

Bennis, W., and P. Beiderman. *Organizing Genius.* (Reading, Mass.: Addison-Wesley, 1997).

Bennis and Beiderman contend the era of the great man (or woman) as leader is over and we are now in the era of great teams. To support their thesis, they narrate case studies of great groups that had a major impact in their field. Among the successful teams chronicled by the authors are the groups that built the atom bomb, the Walt Disney creative team responsible for many of the Disney cartoon characters, the Bill Clinton 1992 election team, and the Xerox group that created the first personal computer. Bennis and Beiderman use each case to tell what makes a great group great.

Cooper, R., and A. Sawaf. *Executive EQ: Emotional Intelligence in Leadership and Organizations.* (New York: Grosset/Putnam, 1997).

The authors of this book also provide specific applications of emotional intelligence skills to leadership. Teaming is a specific focus for their use of EQ in leadership.

Hackman, J., ed. *Groups That Work (and Those That Don't).* (San Francisco: Jossey-Bass, 1990).

Hackman and his fellow authors studied a number of teams, most of which were not successful. The inquiry into why teams fail is instructive for anyone building or leading a team.

LEADERSHIP DEVELOPMENT

The Collaborative Professional Development Process, available from the Council of Chief State School Officers at http://www.ccsso.org.

The Interstate School Leaders Licensure Consortium (ISLLC) recently developed a process for school leaders to develop more effective leadership skills. This Collaborative Professional Development Process is grounded in the ISLLC Standards, the school's improvement plan, and the leadership needs of the principal. The school leader assembles a team to provide honest feedback on the artifacts and leader's reflections about professional growth. This process is consistent with our thinking about professional development and could be a useful tool.

Donmoyer, R., M. Imber, and J. Scheurich, eds. *The Knowledge Base in Educational Administration: Multiple Perspectives*. (Albany, N.Y.: SUNY Press, 1995).

This book provides an overview of the various perspectives on school leadership. The issues and factors the authors discuss provide context for our view of school leadership. This book could be useful to those who want to better understand the issues school leaders face and the issues that support a more individualized approach to the development of school leadership knowledge and skill.

The Jossey-Bass Reader on Educational Leadership. (San Francisco: Jossey-Bass, 2000).

This book contains twenty-four chapters in which some of the most well-known authors in school leadership share their views on a variety of timely leadership topics. These views can help you develop some perspective on the nature of leadership, the kinds of issues that affect situations and constituents, and grounding in the realities of modern school leadership.

McCauley, C., R. Moxley, and E. Van Velsor, eds. *The Center for Creative Leadership Handbook of Leadership Development*. (San Francisco: Jossey-Bass, 1998).

This book further develops the "learning through experience" theme we think is the only meaningful way for leaders to become more effective. The book contains additional information for those who are serious about learning through reflection on the work being done. We recommend this book to you if you need additional details on how to use the analysis of situations, constituents, self-knowledge, and emotional intelligence to plan your development.

Northouse, P. *Leadership: Theory and Practice.* (Thousand Oaks, Calif.: Sage, 2001).

This is one of the best texts we have found on leadership theory. It does a wonderful job of describing the thinking about leadership that has dominated researchers. It can be a useful tool for you if you feel that you need to know more about how leadership theories evolved in order to better understand yourself or your situation.

Ross, L., and R. Nisbett. *The Person and the Situation.* (New York: McGraw-Hill, 1991).

This book explores the relationships between people and situations. It provides insights on our behaviors and how situations affect what we do in unknown ways. This book is a useful tool for those interested in understanding situations more thoroughly.

Senge, P. *The Fifth Discipline: The Art and Practice of the Learning Organization.* (New York: Doubleday, 1995).

This book explores new ways of thinking about organizations. It describes learning organizations and how organizations get better. Systems thinking, personal mastery, mental models, building shared vision, and team learning are themes the author explores in ways that can be enlightening to leaders who seek to better understand situations and followers.

About the Authors

James O. McDowelle has been a teacher, principal, and superintendent in the public schools. From 1965 until 1972, he served as an officer in the United States Army, with tours of duty in Vietnam and the Pentagon. He received the Bronze Star for service in Vietnam. He received his doctorate from the University of Virginia in 1981. Dr. McDowelle has been department chair for departments of educational leadership at Appalachian State University and East Carolina University. He is currently professor and director of the Ph.D. program in the School of Education at Drexel University in Philadelphia, Pennsylvania.

In 1990, Dr. McDowelle received the Roy R. Blanton Award for Excellence in Teaching at Appalachian State University. While serving as a school administrator, he received the Omega Psi Phi "Citizen of the Year" Award in 1987 and the Hopeland Investment Positive Image Award in 1986. In 1995, he was profiled in *The School Administrator.* He is a member of the National Alliance of Black School Educators (Superintendents Division).

Dr. McDowelle is the coauthor with Dr. Patricia A. Miller of *Administration of Preschool Programs in Public Schools* (1993) and editor of *The Principal's Internship Handbook: An Exercise in Praxis* (1997). He is the author of several articles on school leadership, interpersonal skills, and the emotions.

Dr. McDowelle has conducted numerous workshops on the skills of school leadership for teachers, administrators, and school board members. He has been a member of the advisory board of the North

Carolina Charter School Commission. He was chair of North Carolina Professors of Educational Leadership in 1994–1995.

Kermit G. Buckner has been a teacher and school administrator in the public schools of North Carolina. He has also served as a director for the North Carolina Department of Public Instruction and as director of professional development and assessment for the National Association of Secondary School Principals (NASSP). He received his doctorate from the University of North Carolina at Greensboro in 1981. Dr. Buckner has been a professor at East Carolina University since 1998 and became department chair in 2001.

Dr. Buckner served on the Interstate School Leaders Licensure Consortium (ISLLC) and participated in the development of the ISLLC Standards. He also was one of the developers of the Consortium's Collaborative Professional Development Process. Dr. Buckner has conducted professional development training programs for school leaders in all fifty states as well as Australia, Germany, Russia, Canada, and Bermuda.

Dr. Buckner has published in the areas of leadership, leadership development, internships, assessment, and education law. He has written several development programs for school leaders.

Dr. Buckner is also chair of the National Association of Secondary School Principals Principal Preparation Task Force. He has been a presenter at numerous national conventions and has worked with several North Carolina school districts to develop future school leaders, and with the North Carolina Department of Public Instruction on performance-based licensure, the NASSP on school leader assessment and development, and the Council of Chief State School Officers on the professional development of school leaders.